Gone *for* 18 Minutes

To Heaven, To Hell, And Back

TERESA G. SIMMONS

Copyright © 2009 Teresa G. Simmons
All rights reserved.

To contact the author, please email her at gonefor18@gmail.com.

Editorial assistance provided by GoodEditors.com,
http://www.goodeditors.com.

Bulk copies of this book are available at discounted prices through the author.

ISBN: 1-4392-5299-8
ISBN-13: 9781439252994

Visit www.booksurge.com to order additional copies.

To Ronnie

You were the vessel God worked His miracle through

You persisted in spite of how desperate everything looked

To God Be the Glory

Table of Contents

Acknowledgements vii
Foreword xi
Introduction xiii
A Beautiful Day for Milking 1
Off the Right Track and Back On Again 7
Plans for the Birthday Girl 13
The Last Thing I Remember 19
Ronnie Acts and Reacts 25
Emergency Medical Team Report 35
Answered Prayers 39
Who I Saw 45
My Mother, My Friend 49
A Place of Life and a Place of Death 55
In the Doctors' Hands and in God's Hands 63
The Word Begins to Travel 69
That's Why You're Back Here with Us 77
"Your Story Gives Me Goosebumps" 81
I Walk, I Talk, and I Wait 85
…And I Wait Some More 89
"Once Again, We Made It" 101
He Was There All the Time 107
Our Easter Miracle 111

Easter is Still Easter, Even in the Hospital 121
Lord, Get Me Through This 125
What Did It All Mean? 135
"You Betcha I'll Share!" 139
The Milkmaid and Her Husband Speak 143
Time to Tell the Rest of the Story 147
Encouragement from Others Who Have Come Back 151
Let's Throw Away the Crutches 159
What Road Will You Take? 163
Sinner's Prayer 165
Epilogue 167

Acknowledgements

I wrote this book after many promptings from people who heard my story. Often they would encourage me to get my account down in writing to "spread the word." After shrugging off the idea for about a year after my incident, one day a lady came up to me after I had shared my experience. She held out her Bible and said: "I feel so strongly that God wants you to see this." She showed me Habakkuk 2:2: "Write down the vision."

The next day as I was praying, I glanced down at some notes I had written a few weeks earlier. I had jotted down Habakkuk 2:2! Funny thing, I didn't remember the reason I had written that Scripture down. I felt at that moment a strong confirmation from the Lord to write down the series of events that had happened to me just a year earlier.

So I did. But not being a writer, I was not satisfied with the results. I e-mailed my crude manuscript to my cousin's husband Nick Fina and to one of our local evangelists and fellow churchgoer (for lack of a better word) Steve Wingfield. They both encouraged me to prevail upon a professional editor.

After praying about it, I found Carolyn Goss. She has been a blessing to work with. Thank you, Carolyn. You've been so supportive with invaluable suggestions, wisdom and positive input. You've truly been an answer to prayer!

I'll be forever grateful to the EMTs from the Mt. Solon Rescue Squad. You volunteered your valuable time and followed up with concern. I also offer my thanks to the staff with PHI and the crew on the medical helicopter from Weyers Cave. (I list them all in the book.)

I thank the staff in the Trauma Unit at UVA for continuing to work with me even though my prognosis looked hopeless.

To my pastor Ed Heatwole and his wife Eileen: Thanks for being there from the beginning and standing faithfully, praying and giving my family hope. Ed, thank you for standing and praying in the ER that day in spite of the "bad news" the doctors were bringing, and for your continued prayers.

Thanks, Cindy Michael, for your enthusiasm and inspiration as I got my story on paper. Thank you for coming to the hospital with Bert to stand that day and pray with my family.

A special thanks to Cheryl Landis for helping to compile my messy notes and typing from my many handwritten pages. You are a such a blessing and you even did this on your vacation!

Thank you, Sharon Hardy and Peggy Bell, for initially correcting my grammar mistakes in the midst of your already busy schedules.

To my dad, Garland and to my brothers Reggie, Randy, and Carlton, my sisters-in-law Sue, Patty, Kathy, and Dana, a special thank-you and hugs for all your support and prayers and for faithfully coming to the hospital nearly every day.

To my children, Eric, Jared, and Rebecca, as well as Rachel, Whitney and Nate: God richly blessed me with the best kids any mom could ever want! It was such a blessing to know you all were faithfully carrying on the work on the farm when your dad and I couldn't be there.

To my beloved husband, Ronnie: No one but God knows what went on in your mind that day. You kept me alive with your quick thinking and your perseverance even when things looked hopeless. You have encouraged me to write all this down and your patience in allowing me to do this in spite of a very busy life on the farm has meant so much.

And to our Lord and Savior for never leaving my side, for protecting my life and returning me to this earth to "finish my work." I pray that this story ministers to your flock. You sent me back to complete my work and I pray I do just that.

To God be the glory.
Teresa Simmons
May 2009

Foreword

We have known Ronnie and Teresa Simmons for almost ten years now. I have been privileged to have served them as their pastor. They have also been a part of our small group that meets in our home. Because of our common interest, we have always shared a close friendship. We have been a part of most of the stories shared in this book.

I remember the phone call on that fateful day as though it was yesterday. The trip to the University of Virginia Medical Center takes about one hour from our home. I remember pleading with God the whole way to the hospital to spare Teresa's life.

The doctor offered no hope. I began thinking about funeral arrangements. Then God spoke into my heart: "Take this family and boldly approach the throne of grace!" We did. Shortly thereafter, the doctor returned. With his head bowed he said, "These are the things we doctors live for but rarely see! She is showing signs of life!" Almost immediately, we stood and held hands and lifted our voices to God in gratitude and petition.

One of the amazing things that happened was the blending of two stories. Story one was Teresa's account of what she saw and experienced as the patient. Story two was the account of what took place in the family waiting room. In real time, neither knew what the other was experiencing. Later we were able to put the stories together to see the hand of God on earth and the hand of God in heaven. Both were divinely choreographed to perfection.

This is a stirring true story of a person we know. We are eyewitnesses to every detail. God has given Teresa a powerful desire to share the accounts of this experience with everyone she meets. And God has opened many doors for her to share that story. Many have recommitted their life to Christ, some for the first time and others who have strayed away from a personal relationship with Jesus. Teresa is a living testimony of a supernatural miracle from a compassionate God.

To God be the glory!
Ed Heatwole
Pastor, New Beginnings Church, Bridgewater, Virginia

Introduction

On Monday, April 10, 2006, I died and went to heaven.

What an affirmation of God's existence, you might say. It is, and I want to share all about it. But there is something else I must relate, too: On the same trip out of this life, as I lay on the ground before the EMTs were able to revive me, my heart having stopped keeping me alive, God also allowed me to view another scene. When I came back to consciousness, the memory of it was frightening and yet had the stamp of truth on it. I saw the opposite of heaven. You might call it hell; it seemed like it was. Whatever it was, it was real.

This book is my story of passing from life into death and back into life again. It is also more than that—I offer my experiences in hopes and confidence that they may turn you from doubt to faith, or if you are already a believer in the God of the ages, that they will give you cause for thankfulness and celebration.

Please come back in time with me now, as I place us on a farm near the Blue Ridge Mountains on a day that changed my life. I hope it changes yours, as well. Ready?

A Beautiful Day for Milking

Monday morning, April 10, 2006, was crisp and cool. As I did every morning, I finished the last of my big mug of robust coffee, quietly slipped down the steps to the mud room, put on my barn clothes, and headed out the door with our two farm dogs, Yona and Amaya.

"Let's go, girls." Tails wagging, they raced me to the door.

I stood at the top of the hill for a moment, quietly taking in the view of the Blue Ridge Mountains near our home. From the hilltop I could see below me animals and buildings that reminded me of miniatures from a child's play set—chickens pecking at their feed, cows meandering in for milking as farmers' wives like me called to them, barns with their round silo roofs and churches with their steeples peeking up below adjacent hilltops. I heard the sounds of morning, as the strutting banty roosters crowed to their hens and cows mooed softly in the distance. Raising livestock and poultry and doing dairy farming were ways of life for most of our neighbors and friends. The scene was beautiful and familiar, and I looked forward to the day ahead.

We live in a unique house, or shall I say, barn, on a dairy farm that consists of 200 gently rolling acres, 40 of them woodlands. We also rent another 270 acres. Our buildings are nestled in the middle of the 200 acres on a wooded hilltop. Our living quarters are on the second story of our house while our horse barn is on the bottom. The mud room, just what the name implies, collects all the dirt the farmers bring in as they enter the house. As we exit this room, we walk right out into the horse barn.

The stalls in the horse barn are home to our younger son's training horses. As I entered the barn, they quietly raised their heads in anticipation of hay. I bid them, "Good Morning," and mounted the farm's other mode of transportation, our four-wheeler. Yona jumped on the back with me just as she did every morning. I slid the barn doors open and descended the graveled driveway to our dairy barn.

Yona wagged her tail in glee, while Amaya ran beside us. They loved this early morning adventure. Anxiously awaiting squirrels scurrying across the driveway, they were constantly on watch. It was going to be a beautiful spring day.

I got to the bottom of the hill and climbed off the four-wheeler to go into the dairy barn. I opened the doors to allow the gentle Holsteins to enter. Their big, soft eyes watched my every move as I methodically went through the routine of getting the milking equipment ready. Generally, all of the cows will not come into the barn from the field, but the few that were standing outside the barn prepared to come on in.

I walked back out and got on the four-wheeler again to bring in the rest of "the girls." Yona loved this part. There were usually rabbits stirring in the early morning hours. She knew this and began wagging her tail and smiling one of those "doggie smiles." We went out a little way and passed through the first gate. I had to stop momentarily. The spring morning was gorgeous! The little song birds had once again returned from their winter homes, and their singing echoed through the trees.

Our Shenandoah Valley stretches 200 miles across the Blue Ridge and Allegheny Mountains. Agriculture is a rich part of its history—it was called "The Breadbasket of the Confederacy" during the Civil War. It averages a growing season of six months. The views from our farm are both peaceful and stunning. On a pleasant morning or evening, often we witness whitetail deer grazing their way from one woodlands to another. Our nighttime sky—"Shenandoah" is believed to mean "daughter of the stars" in the old Senedos Indian language—is something you don't see in the city, where the brightness of urban lights diminishes the view of the heavens; out at our farm we can look up and marvel at millions of twinkling stars as we stand in awe of God's creation.

As I looked over the land and beyond once again and saw the sun rising over the Blue Ridge mountains, I knew how the psalmist must have felt in Psalm 148:7-13: "Praise the Lord from the earth...you mountains and all hills...wild animals and all cattle, small creatures and flying birds... young men and maidens, old men and children. Let them praise the name of the Lord." I breathed it all in. "God, you are so good!" I quietly whispered to Him.

As I continued across the field, a warm breeze blew as though God was gently acknowledging me. Funny how unusually close I felt to Him this morning. I never dreamed what He was about to do in my life.

I rounded up the rest of the herd and slowly drove them into the barn. Closing the gate behind them, I whistled for Yona. She came running into the barn to see what left-over milk awaited her. Amaya had gone back to the house already.

Routine milking was relatively new for me. Until the last four years, I had been primarily a housewife running to our children's various activities. Once they had all graduated, I had picked up a couple of part-time jobs working for friends who owned businesses, one in a coffee shop and the other in a kitchenware store.

The jobs were enjoyable, but the hours were limited and the work didn't bring in a lot of revenue. Meanwhile, my husband Ronnie was becoming tired and discouraged. We asked a local agriculture extension agent to come out to our farm to give his opinion on how to improve the farm's finances and lighten the load for Ronnie. He saw the signs of fatigue that Ronnie's heavy workload was causing, and he suggested my giving up the part-time jobs since they really weren't bringing in a lot of money. That way I'd be able to concentrate more on the farm.

The agent thought that I should help with some of the milking in order to give Ronnie a break. I began doing most of the morning milking and calf feeding. Later, we hired Ronnie's nephew to help.

While Ronnie's workload was relieved, there was still lots to do. I found myself thinking a lot about how Ronnie had done this for years without much help. His father came often and helped whenever he could, but still the pressure of managing a farm was always on Ronnie's shoulders. Even though milking wasn't one of the most glorious jobs, I knew it gave Ronnie some extra time to get other things done. I think this was what kept me doing it.

I cut the milk pump on and began putting the automatic milkers on the cows in the barn. As I worked I found myself thinking about other things, as well. On this particular day we would be celebrating our youngest child, Rebecca's, birthday. She would be turning twenty-three. She had asked her father and me if we could host a backyard barbecue for her and some friends. While farming is a busy occupation, we enjoy breaking away from it occasionally to celebrate life's events. I had remembered the night before to marinate the pork that we planned to cook over the open charcoal pit. I also tried to make mental notes of all that I wanted to prepare for the birthday bash.

Occasionally, I let my mind come back to the job at hand. The "girls" gently chewed their cuds while I washed their udders and put on the milkers. The hum of the pump that kept the whole operation running drowned out most other noises.

Again, my mind started drifting. I thought back to how long we'd been dairy farmers. For twenty-six years this had been our livelihood. Together, Ronnie and I had raised three children on the farm. Our oldest son, Eric, was planning to marry his lovely fiancée, Rachel, in September. Our middle son, Jared, was dating a cute little brunette who was ready to go off to college for her master's degree, while Rebecca had finally found the love of her life. Each child had a soul mate and seemed happy.

As I had done many times before, I began thinking about the future of our occupation. Did we want to continue dairy farming now that we had raised our family? The milk market had been spiraling downward for some time, and we weren't seeing a lot of profit. Farming was getting tough.

I began asking God my hard questions: "Where do you want us, God? If you want us to do something different, please give us some direction." I had often struggled with the stigma some people attached to farming. It would have been so easy to walk away from it.

I went even deeper with my thinking. "God, am I doing what you want me to do? Am I glorifying you?" I thought back to when our church was reading Rick Warren's book, *Purpose Driven Life*. He has the reader ask, "Are you glorifying God in what you do?"

At the time I was reading it, I had wondered how I, as a milkmaid, could bring glory to God. For three hours twice a day we were in the barn with one hundred cows, getting milk from them and then spending the remaining time cleaning up after them and feeding the baby calves. I had to ask, "God, how can that bring you glory?"

God has such a sense of humor! As I had read on a few pages later, there it was, tucked away, a quote I'll never forget: "Even a milkmaid can bring glory to God."

I think God had inspired Rick Warren to put that in his book just for me. Interestingly, on this particular morning, I found myself asking the question again. Little did I know how He was about to answer me in a very big way.

Off the Right Track and Back On Again

Before I knew it, I was halfway through the milking. I like to take a little break about then, so I slipped over to the barn office. This is the room where my husband keeps records on the herd, making notes on everything from the time they are bred, when they have their babies, and what their feed rations are. Since some of the medicine that we occasionally give to the cows needs to be kept cool, a refrigerator is in this office. It also stashes snacks, orange juice, water and yes, milk too. I took a big swig of orange juice, grabbed a handful of peanuts off the desk, glanced at the clock on the wall and figured I had better hurry. We had a party to plan and prepare.

I walked back in with the cows and began preparing the next group to be milked. I could almost do this job blindfolded. Again, I let my mind wander to keep from fretting more over all that still had to be done.

Here I was, a forty-eight-year-old milkmaid. I have often thought back to many conversations and plans I had with my best friend, Donna, in high school. We had dreamed about our weddings. We would go to the library and gaze in awe at the beautiful models and wedding gowns in the bridal magazines. There we would discuss what kind of houses we would live in and we would pick out our dream homes from magazines such as *Better Homes and Gardens*.

We were two young teenage girls making such elaborate plans. Donna was such an interesting friend, very pretty, popular and smart. When we first got together as friends, I knew there was something different about her. She didn't follow the crowd. She talked a lot about her church. I could just sense the excitement in her voice when she discussed prayer, her pastor, and the music they played. I wanted to be just like her.

I was raised in a mainstream denominational church, a good church. I would often see my dad early in the morning praying by his bedside. My mother would talk to me about doing things that would please Jesus, but it didn't connect. I didn't know how I could talk to or do for someone that I didn't know. Somehow that Jesus was just a picture in my Sunday School books. I didn't know Him.

Yet, here was my friend Donna coming to school each day excited about what this Jesus was doing in her life, how He had healed someone in her church, and how gigantic prayers were being answered. I would get excited just hearing her talk about it. What I didn't know was that the Holy Spirit was preparing me. He was planting a growing desire for Jesus in my life, gently wooing me to Him. I thought it was Donna I wanted to be like, but I saw Jesus reflected in her life, and really, that is what I wanted. I just didn't know that.

I jumped at the chance when she invited me one night to church. I really wanted to see what all the excitement was about. I packed a change of clothes and headed off to school that day with the intention of going home with Donna and then to church.

Many times before, my family had driven by this little country church nestled right against the Allegheny Mountains, but this would be the first time I had entered its doors. As I walked in, I could feel it. This is exactly what I felt when Donna would excitedly share what was happening in her life. It was He. It was the Holy Spirit. It was Jesus. I had never felt anything like this before.

Two of Donna's older friends were singing and playing guitars. I had never seen a guitar in church, only an organ and piano. This music was so different. They were singing, with deep meaning behind the words. I stood there truly amazed.

I had not necessarily been a "bad girl," but somehow, I felt right then and there that I wanted to be changed. I wanted to be different from how I was. I didn't understand the hunger I felt, a hunger for something deep and fulfilling.

After everyone greeted each other with hugs and smiles, we were all seated. Donna's pastor stood in front of us and spoke about a love that only God the Father can give. He spoke tenderly of a Father somehow here on this earth that could just take us, embrace us, and make us feel different from what we ever had felt before. There it was. That word—*different*. That was what I wanted!

I don't remember all the words he spoke that night, but I remember the tears. The tears were on his face, the tears were on Donna's face, and on everyone's faces around me. And then they were rolling down my own face. Somehow I was being changed already.

Donna's two friends began playing the soft music that had greeted me when I walked in the door. As I saw others going forward to the altar, I knew that was the only place for me right then. Somehow, that was where it could all take place. As I knelt at the altar that evening, I was enveloped with something I had never felt before. It truly did feel as if God took me gently in His arms, warmly embraced me, and whispered in my ear that He loved me.

Something very different took place that night. My life would never be the same. His love and forgiveness is just like that—life-changing. There I was—different! What I had thought was all about Donna actually had been all about Him. Our lives can really reflect His glory. I was on top of cloud nine! I couldn't wait to share.

I am so glad Donna and I were young teenagers when this happened. We were unbridled with enthusiasm. As a result, I went to school and shared Christ's love and invited others to church.

I was a runner on the track team, and I talked and prayed to God as I ran. I loved it! I would run through our woods on little packed-dirt paths and pour my heart out to God. I asked Him over and over, "Have I done anything that is not pleasing to you?" I just wanted to be close to Him. I wanted nothing to separate me from Him.

In my family's church I had opportunities to participate in lay witness missions. I went along with a group of people to other churches, where we gave testimonies about our lives to people we'd never met. Those times were some of the best in all my teenage years.

I remember opening up the window on our old two story farm house and praying for hours at night. I somehow could picture God in heaven looking down at me, listening to me. The closeness was incredible. I had a little paperback New Testament, a *Good News for Modern Man*, a translation in contemporary English, that made the Bible live for me. I highlighted the pages so much that I eventually had to buy a second one.

And yet. . .I was a teenager, after all. There are many varieties of temptation that seem attractive when a person is young and unaware of the long-term consequences of wrong choices. I started riding to an after-school job with a girl in school who was one of the ones with the "reputation." I did not realize how bad company can put to ruins the best intentions. I went down hill fast!

I started hanging out with all the wrong kids. A school friend noticed me with my new-found friends and commented to me, "Teresa, I didn't know you were like that!" The same window I once raised and prayed to God out of, I would now raise and smoke cigarettes out of. I'm sure this was a shock to my parents.

In fact, I know it was. Years later I asked my dad, "How did you handle us going through rotten times (each of us kids had those times)?

He answered, "Teresa, I knelt by my bedside window and would pray each night that God would protect each of you and would bring you each home safely, and you know He did just that."

God did do that, and He went beyond that. He brought each of us home, and each of us is a Christian today.

I began to return to God when I was in my early twenties, and I was again in a close relationship with Him by the time Mom died. Today I realize that God had remembered those earlier years, my first love. He was a patient and merciful God, waiting on me.

Many times since then I have reflected on the early days of my relationship with God. As I look back, I've seen a road that at times took wrong directions. Various choices I made in life threw me off the track. However, God in his unfathomable love, again gently brought me back to Him.

Plans for the Birthday Girl

The soft mooing of the Holsteins returned me to the present as I urged them into the barn to be fed. Before I knew it, I was seeing the last of the cows coming into the barn. I would not be long now. I could get to the house, cook, clean, and bake a birthday cake.

As I was finishing the last few cows, I felt my heart fluttering. I had been experiencing this quite a bit lately. And the fatigue! I had been drinking a lot of coffee as a quick-fix solution for it, but deep down I knew the coffee was not good for the heart palpitations I was experiencing. I felt sometimes as if my heart was going to jump out of my chest. Oh well, I had too much going on to worry about that, I thought. We had a birthday party to plan.

I saw the last of "the girls" exiting the barn, swishing their tails as though to say goodbye. I sprayed the barn down with the high-powered pressure hose and began getting some milk ready for the baby calves.

We had around twenty-five babies to feed. As cute as they are, this is usually an undesirable job on any dairy farm. It often falls on the wife to take care of the calves. Guess it is just part of that nurturing spirit we as women are supposed to have.

I pulled the Rubbermaid cart around to the door of the dairy barn and loaded the buckets of milk. The calves' hutches were not too far away. They heard the cart coming their way and began a chorus of "Mmmaaa," which sounds just like they are saying "Ma." Some of the older ones had been trained to sip their milk from plastic gallon tubs, while the younger ones drank from two quart bottles. This can be a very mundane job—but the routine of it day after day can make it and other sometimes tedious chores good times to think and pray.

I often think God's heart is especially near the farm. In fact, it is in this setting that I often feel very close to Him. Here I receive answers to prayers. Nature is all around. I felt particularly close to God this April morning, though I had no idea what was about to take place. My heart fluttered again and again I consoled myself, "OK, OK. Just cut back on the coffee."

I finished the feeding. Time to find Yona, get on the four-wheeler, and head back to the house. Yona was eager to get on and to go back to learn what Amaya was up to.

The birthday girl was still in bed. Good! I figured. I had time to fix one of her favorites: pumpkin bars. Before I did this I needed to start the charcoal so that my husband could grill the meat. Everyone would be coming early in the evening, so I wanted to allow lots of time for it to cook. I found my husband not too far away, feeding the horses.

Ronnie has always had a love for horses. I discovered this when we first started dating. He owned three then. After we started a family, time and money were limited and the horses had to be sold. Ronnie vowed he would one day own some again, and he kept that promise to himself. When our second son turned nine, he also became very enthusiastic about horses. I think he collected every plastic horse model that was made. When that novelty died, it was time for the real thing.

We would often see a black horse running up on a hillside behind our church. Little did we know, the man who owned it also did our nutrition planning for our dairy cows. When we discovered this, there was no holding back; this black horse, named Clim, had to be ours! Even more amazing, he was for sale!

How exciting for our nine-year-old son, Jared! Jared had loved horses since as far back as I can remember. He used to say, "I want to be a horse when I grow up," so I made him a little horse costume that he'd wear, "galloping" around the farm. We bought Clim, and he was immediately like a new member of the family. He was special, so much that the kids would make him cakes of grain, caramel, and apples for his birthday.

We soon discovered one horse just would not go around for five members of the family. It wasn't long before another horse was purchased and brought to the farm, then another, and another. . . . My husband's own love for horses was fueled by our son's desire to own more. We now have about twenty horses for the different family members to ride.

For dairy farmers, vacation time is limited. We found that horseback riding in our beautiful surrounding mountains on a Sunday afternoon almost every week topped one week of vacation time. We discovered Dave, an older man in our community who also loved riding and loved sharing stories he had learned while growing up around our beloved mountains and countryside. How much fun to rush home after church on Sunday, pack sandwiches and drinks, load the horses and kids, and head for the mountains with our new friend! I think he was just as excited. Each time we rode we would wonder what new and different place and story he would treat us with. It was always somewhere different, and the stories intrigued us and entertained the kids. He always knew the sunny spots along the trails to dismount and eat lunch.

We would remove the saddlebags and pass out sandwiches and drinks. Dave would snap open his can of Vienna sausage and pork-n-beans, and we would sit, talk, and dream while the horses would quietly stand nearby, swishing off flies with their tails, their eyes half closed. "Well, if we're going to find our way back to the trailer before dark, we'd better get back on the trail," he'd say. By then, everyone was fed and rested and ready to discover what else remained unseen ahead.

We'd go on these trail rides nearly every season but winter. It was always hard to tell which season was prettiest from the mountain top. How I missed those days! As the kids got older, these adventures were replaced with others.

However, the love of horses never stopped, especially for Jared. Eric went on to train as a draftsman in a local engineering company. Though he had limited time to ride, he still enjoyed horses. Rebecca occasionally rode with friends. But for Jared, horses became not just a passion but a profession. Upon graduating from high school, he attended an equestrian training school, and once he graduated from that, he began a horse training business on the farm. Many horse owners brought their animals to the farm for training, so many that sometimes we weren't sure unless we counted them whether we were keeping more horses or more cows.

I could usually find my husband or my son with the horses, either feeding them or just stroking their shiny coats while they would just quietly stand. Some special unspoken communication must exist between a horse lover and his horse. It is as if they just understand one another. Ever hear of the horse whisperer? I would often witness this when my husband or son would be around horses. There is a unique relationship that takes place. I would at times envy it.

On this particular lovely April Monday morning, after finding my husband near the horses, I coaxed him to come and put the pork over the charcoal to get it done before the guests arrived. He reluctantly walked away from his beloved horses.

I went back into the house and showered off the barn dirt. After blow drying my hair, the alarm clock caught my eye. Still lots to be done. I tried to ignore the fluttering going on in my heart again. Feeling as if I needed a boost to get me going, I went into the kitchen and put on another pot of my favorite robust coffee. While it was brewing, I started the batter for the pumpkin bars. I rarely made them, but today was special. They would be a splurge for Rebecca's breakfast.

For some unknown reason, I began to feel unusually good. I still do not know why. When my husband came into the house to get the meat forks to turn the meat, I commented to him about my new-found energy. It was almost too good to be true, considering how fatigued I normally felt. And this was even before drinking the coffee that was perking. Thinking nothing of it, I began mixing a batter of red velvet cake. This was going to be a feast!

Why did I feel like going to such extremes for our kids? I sometimes tried to answer that question to myself. While my brothers and I were growing up, finances were tight. Our parents had lived through the depression in the '30s, they had seen hard times, and our family never did have much in material riches. I used to often think we were poor. I recognize now what we did have was riches in love, but when Ronnie and I had our own kids I sometimes got a little carried away with trying to make sure they didn't feel deprived. But skimp on food? I loved to cook and bake. I guess it is just the farm girl in me. Let's spread the old wooden table with a farm feast!

The red velvet cake went into the oven while the pumpkin bars came out. I needed to get some side dishes prepared before long. As I walked by the window, I glanced at the grass in our backyard. Boy, did it need mowing! Rebecca's friends were going to be hanging out here. What a shabby looking lawn!

I peeked in her bedroom to see if "Birthday Girl" was stirring yet. Knowing I wouldn't have time to mow first, I decided to ice the pumpkin bars, get her a mug of the fresh coffee, and greet her by her bedside with a favorite treat.

I got it all prepared just in time. As my sleepy twenty-three-year-old opened her eyes, I plastered a good morning kiss on her cheek and wished her a happy birthday. Her eyes opened really wide when she saw the pumpkin bars. "Thanks, Mom!" I felt as though she was five again. I thought, why do we have to let our kids grow up?

She said she needed to run into town with her boyfriend for a little while, and I told her I would be out mowing. "Be back soon!" I yelled as I put my Nike flip-flops on to go mow. I had just taken the cake out to cool while I was mowing. The other dishes would have to wait a little while.

The Last Thing I Remember

As I once again walked out of the mud room into the horse barn, I saw the horses had just been fed. Jared had started his daily chores while I was still at the barn milking. I had been preoccupied getting things ready for "Birthday Girl" and hadn't greeted him.

I walked around and found Jared mucking one of the horse stalls. "Good morning, Son."

He mumbled "Good morning" back; he was busy doing his chores.

I said, "See you later," and got on with the work that was waiting.

I once again hopped on the four-wheeler to ride down the hill to the barn where we kept the mowing tractor. I would have to leave it parked at the barn while I took the tractor up to mow around the house. I transferred rides.

I mowed along the driveway around the big oak trees while making my way up to the top. Breathing in the fresh mowed grass, I just had to bask in that moment. Getting a whiff of the charcoal smoke coming from behind the house, sniffing in the Christmas aroma from our cedar trees nearby–life could not get any better. I was absorbing every good thing in that hour.

"God, you are truly amazing!" I whispered to Him, while the humming motor of the riding tractor purred. He was preparing something huge! If I had had any idea. . .

As I got the front yard mowed, I realized I needed to get quickly around to the backyard and finish it as well. I would have to do this carefully because this is where my beloved husband was charcoaling the meat.

He was patiently sitting in one of the lawn chairs as I approached the corner of the house on the mower. He was in his own little world watching the meat cook.

While we were dating, Ronnie and I would often come up to this hilltop, and he would tell me how he wanted one day to build a house here. I would secretly dream in my heart that I would be his wife and that we would live here together. God does give us the desires of our hearts. And here I am, I thought once again.

The mower buzzed around trees and flower beds, and I was off in my thinking, planning what flowers I would plant this year, when suddenly the mower sputtered. I turned off the key quickly.

Glancing up, I saw a look of concern in my husband's eyes. This was a diesel and diesels should never run out of fuel. I had not even checked the fuel gauge. Such a "woman" thing to do! I assured him I would get fuel and that I had turned it off just in time.

What we did not know was that the tractor was not out of fuel. It was low, but not out. We still do not know why it sputtered, but my husband turned the key on later and it started right away. We were experiencing God's perfect timing, but we did not know that until later.

We have a fuel pump at the barn, which would mean I would have to walk down that hill, fill up a can with diesel fuel, and bring it back up. Oh well, I had the energy that day.

I grabbed a fuel can from our garden tool room near the horse stalls and was accompanied down the hill by good old faithful Yona. When I got near the fuel pumps, I realized then I had left the four-wheeler nearby and could just ride it up. As I got on, I heard our nephew Devin nearby. He was our right-hand man on the farm, the only son of my husband's sister. He loved farming and had been helping us on the farm for about a year. We could always depend on Devin. He asked if he could ride up to the house with me as he had a question for his Uncle Ronnie.

Have you ever done something and then wondered later why you did it? Well, this was one of those moments. I got off the four-wheeler and convinced Devin that I needed the exercise. "Take it on up, I'll walk." He has always been a thoughtful boy and argued I should ride, too. I assured him I'd be all right. He went on while I stood there in amazement at what I'd just said I'd do. "Why did I just say that? Oh well, the exercise will do me good," I told myself.

We often don't know how God is working in our lives. I had declined that ride for a reason, but I didn't know it at the time.

All the fluttering I had been experiencing in my heart had been diagnosed by my medical doctor as *PVCs,* premature ventricular contractions. I had been told they were benign, nothing to worry about. What we didn't know was that there was a genetic disorder in my heart. An irregular rhythm could be triggered by exercise and switch into a lethal rhythm without warning.

Such had been the case of my youngest brother, Mark. We were four years apart in age, but had grown up in a very close relationship. Our mother had died when Mark was only twenty-four and I was twenty-eight. I was married then with our three children, whereas Mark had no one. I felt at times as if I had stepped into his life as a mother, cooking him meals, cleaning, and just taking care of him.

Mark eventually married and had four children. He and his wife, Dana, took a trip to Tennessee in the fall of 2004 to celebrate their wedding anniversary. Their four children, ages four, eleven, fourteen and fifteen, were anxiously awaiting their return on October 18, a day none of us will forget.

I received a phone call from his distressed wife early that morning. She tearfully shared how Mark had had what she thought was a heart attack. They were far from medics. He had collapsed around 6:00 a.m. and she had tried CPR unsuccessfully. The first person to the scene was a policeman. EMTs arrived later. Dana was hurriedly packing up their things so she could get to the medical center where they had taken him. I notified my other brothers. We were all anxious to hear from her. I received a dreaded phone call a little while later.

I screamed as I heard her words, "Mark didn't make it."

"No, No, No!" I kept yelling into the phone. "This must be a bad dream. He's too young!"

We had lost our mother when she was sixty-six years old. The doctors had told us our mother had an arrhythmia and congestive heart failure. Her heart was the size of a cantaloupe. The news was devastating to us all. Eighteen months later she died. We witnessed our dad's grief as he had to say goodbye to his mate of forty-three years. I had lost not only my mother but my best friend then.

And there I was once more, saying good-bye to a brother that I had taken under my wing and somehow was supposed to nurture since Mom had left this earth. He was only forty-two. The trauma was too great. Seeing his children's faces when they were told their daddy wouldn't be coming home was greater sorrow than anything else I could ever bear. My grieving dad took them each into his arms and told them what had happened. This is an image that's very hard to recall. It's like a tender wound in the emotions that just triggers the tears. I try not to think about it. Seeing Mark's wife Dana pick up the pieces and carry on has been hard.

We never had an autopsy done. The death certificate listed ventricular fibrillation as the cause of death. My brother's death did alert each of us to have some routine heart examination done. None of the tests revealed anything alarming, though mine did show the PVCs that I was feeling as I walked up the hill. "Lots of people have these; nothing to be concerned about," my medical doctor had said.

Most mornings I would have been alone when I experienced what I thought were PVCs. This particular day my heart went into ventricular tachycardia, a dangerous and potentially fatal condition of very fast and sometimes irregular heartbeats. My husband and nephew "just happened" to be around. I would realize later how perfect God's timing is.

As I climbed the hill carrying the fuel can, I wasn't even thinking about my heart; I was feeling much too good. I was just wishing I would have this energy all the time. No signs, no premonition surfaced that a life-changing event was about to take place. Once I got to the top of the hill, I walked around to the back of the house, still carrying the diesel fuel. I could hear my husband and nephew talking. I smelled the inviting aroma of charcoal and heard the meat crackling as it cooked.

Then suddenly, I didn't feel right. I began getting dizzy. Fearful that I would fall, I crouched down with my hands on my knees. Then the nausea came. I commented to Devin, "I think that hill got to me."

He replied, "Maybe it's the heat."

I had to move away, fearing I would get sick in front of them. A few yards over stood a hitching rail my husband had built. I stood up, made my way to it, and put my forearm down on it for support. That's the last thing I can remember.

Ronnie Acts and Reacts

I saw the helicopter landing on Ronnie and Teresa's farm and I dropped my chores and rushed over. When I saw Teresa, she was blue and unconscious. I thought she was already gone.
—Carlton Simmons

I was out on a trail ride. My cousin Devin was working for my dad. He came and got me. He said, "You may wanna get on up there. Your mom, she's collapsed and I'm going down to make sure the ambulances know where to turn in." I ran up the driveway, tied up the horse, and went over to her on the ground. When I saw her I felt there was very little hope. My dad was crying and immediately I began praying. Lord please be with her, please help her. Her face was blue but she was making groaning noises like she was kind of there so I thought, maybe there is a little hope, but I just kept praying until the ambulances got there. Then they started working on her and there were a lot of things going through my mind. I was really scared at that time but then after they airlifted her for some reason I got a peace about it all.

At that time I called my brother and my sister. Of course I was shook up but there was this peace. I think they had kind of stabilized her by that time but I think the peace was more the Lord saying, "This is gonna be OK."
—Jared Simmons

My husband saw me on the ground. He didn't fully realize what had happened yet. When he saw Yona licking my face, he knew I had to be out—I never let a dog lick me on the face. Ronnie jumped up and came running over. I was already blue. He thought right away about heart problems. I had been voicing my concern about the frequent palpitations I had been experiencing. Ronnie remembered what had happened with Mark and went into action immediately.

Being a quick thinker, Ronnie got down and started compressions on my chest. He breathed in my mouth and then continued with strong compressions. He had never learned how to do CPR—but something, or more accurately some *One*, must have given him an instant lesson, because we learned later that his quick reaction time saved my life.

Many things went through his mind as he worked on me. He thought, "She will never see her grandchildren." He forcefully pushed on my chest and blew again into my mouth.

"Devin, call 911!" he yelled. Time seemed to stand still for them. Though Devin placed the call at 1:29 and the EMS squad arrived only 18 minutes later, Ronnie later said it felt as if it were an eternity until they got to our house. He methodically pushed hard and puffed big breaths into my lungs. Meanwhile Jared, who was training one of the horses, got word of what was happening. He told me later, "Mom, you were so blue. All I could think about was Uncle Mark."

"Where is the rescue squad?!" Ronnie shouted. Push, push, push. Blow a breath again. He didn't even know if he was making any progress.

Devin took the four-wheeler down to the driveway's entrance to flag the rescue squad. The call alerted a father and son team who were mowing grass at a church almost ten minutes away. Roger Kiracofe and his son Jeremy quickly jumped into their vehicle and headed our way. The local rescue squad was leaving the squad building, also around ten minutes away.

Roger and Jeremy arrived first, and much to Ronnie's relief, took over with CPR. Jeremy then did something that amazed everyone.

Generally, when a "working code" (such as I was) is in progress, an aircraft is not called to the scene. For some reason, Jeremy felt prompted to call our local medical helicopter. When the EMTs later asked Jeremy why he made that call, he replied, "I really don't know why I did it." But it was the right call, and a helicopter was immediately dispatched. There were lots of other unexplained events that day. Jeremy later told me that while he was administering CPR my eyes were opened at times as if looking at him, but he knew I saw nothing. He said he couldn't sleep for two nights after that.

I was without a pulse and not breathing when the EMTs arrived. I was a "code blue," in cardiac arrest—*clinically dead*, but not pronounced dead yet—the EMTs would do all they could do to resuscitate me before the official time of death would be called, if it came to that. They hooked a defibrillator to my chest. When the device advised a shock, they administered one.

One of the EMTs, Kitty Pitsenbarger, is a registered nurse at our local hospital. Days later, she told me that prior to the first shock, my heart was in ventricular fibrillation, or "V-fib." In this emergency condition, there is uncoordinated contraction of the cardiac muscle of the ventricles in the heart, making them tremble rather than contract properly. If the arrhythmia continues for more than a few seconds, blood circulation will cease, and death can occur in a matter of minutes. Without a defibrillator, life cannot be sustained.

After the first shock, my heart went into pulseless electrical activity, or "P.E.A." Kitty explained to me what this term means. A P.E.A. occurs when the heart shows electrical activity but no pulse is felt. No blood is being sent through the body. She told me she had never seen anyone pull through that. Later, when I asked a cardiologist the chances of surviving P.E.A., he told me less than five percent survive.

Kitty also informed me of other conditions that took place. She explained what a "working code" is, and said that in a rural setting such as ours, only .02 percent, *two-hundredths of one percent*, survive. Talk about slim chances! She told me for some "unexplained" reason my heart went from the P. E. A. into ventricular tachycardia, a dangerous coronary event in which my heart was beating more than two hundred beats a minute—this kind of arrhythmia can result in sudden death. The defibrillator advised another shock. Again, my heart went into ventricular tachycardia. Upon the third shock, I was given Lidocaine, a heart regulating medicine.

Now here's another "unexplained" aspect of the day: it is not always the case that a cardiac tech is available to come on a call in our small community. We have a tech who volunteers his time with our local rescue squad and comes on calls when he can, but he's not always able to because he also works as a fireman in a nearby town. He came on the call to our farm that day. He happened to be off from his regular job.

Meanwhile someone directed the helicopter crew to land in one of our fields. The helicopter set down in our pasture at 2:05 p.m. The EMTs were already preparing my body for the flight. At various times I remember barely coming to. I could hear everyone talking, but it was like hearing through water. I would see flashes. People were moving past me and then I felt my body being jostled around.

Three disturbing memories remain in my fuzzy recollections of those minutes. One, I remember vividly the shocks the EMTs administered. I felt the tremendous pain and pressure as the shocks sent strong jolts into my body. Whatever state of being I was in, I remember praying to Jesus, "Please don't let them kill me." My mind could not fully rationalize what was occurring. All I knew was that I felt pain. I also remember the frustration I experienced in not being able to respond. It was like a bad dream from which I was trying to get awake. When I would occasionally come to, I would try to communicate with them, but to no avail. I felt so helpless. The third thing I remember thinking is, this is my daughter's birthday. I can't die on her birthday!

Once the EMTs got my body ready for the flight in the helicopter to UVA Hospital in Charlottesville, an hour's drive away, my husband and son grabbed the horses and tried to keep them calm while the huge craft lifted off the ground and flew right over. I think the temporary distraction somehow helped them not to think about the bleakness of that hour. God only knows what must have been going through their minds as they saw the helicopter ascend over the Blue Ridge Mountains.

At some point my brother Carlton, a beef and turkey farmer who lives nearby, saw the helicopter land on our farm. He told me later that lots of thoughts ran through his mind. Had our son been injured while training horses? Had my husband been injured in an accident on our farm? Or had something happened to my father-in-law? He raced up our driveway in his pickup. Thinking he would see EMTs working with someone else, he was dismayed to see them working on his sister—my blond hair was the first thing he spotted. His mind flashed back to our brother Mark. "No, God! Not someone else in our family!" he pleaded. He couldn't bring himself too close. A quiet, gentle person, he stood back and prayed.

My husband and son knew there would be an hour's trip ahead of them to Charlottesville. They ran into the house and called the other two children to alert them and then began getting ready for the ride across the mountain.

On the way, my husband knew best how to use this time—phone calls could be made, prayers could and should be started. He called our pastor, a strong praying warrior. It was as if a spark had ignited a wild fire. Phones were buzzing all around. My loved ones, friends, neighbors, and fellow churchgoers were lifting their voices to heaven, pleading to a merciful God to spare my life.

I remember at one point "coming to" in the helicopter. I could hear the loud sounds coming from the motor. I tried to identify what I was hearing and where I was. I could hear voices, but not of anyone I knew. They were the EMTs that flew the chopper. Where was I? What is going on? I wondered. I remember a strange feeling—I felt so calm. It was strange and wonderful at the same time. I thought to myself, I don't know where I am, but it doesn't matter because I feel so tranquil.

That was the last thought I had before my body went into cardiogenic shock, which is a leading cause of death after a heart attack. Kitty later explained this medical term to me. *Cardiogenic shock* happens when the heart does not pump blood efficiently and blood and fluid begin backing up into the lungs. I was also losing oxygen. To make matters worse, while I was being resuscitated, I had aspirated my lunch into my lungs. Stomach contents just are not supposed to be in the lungs. Chemically, the lining of my lungs was being burned.

Today I stand in awe of how I had been without a pulse, not breathing—in short, clinically dead, and am now alive. I escaped the point of no return. I was told eighty percent of people die when they go into cardiogenic shock. The way I figure it is that I went from a *.02 percent chance* of surviving a code, to a five percent chance of surviving pulseless electrical activity of the heart, to a twenty percent chance of surviving cardiogenic shock. My chances were climbing, but barely.

What normally takes an hour by car to get to this hospital took the helicopter twelve minutes. Upon arriving, the crew took me off and into the emergency room where the trauma team began working on me. My systolic blood pressure was 43. (It's normally 118). Things did not look good at all. One of the male nurses on the trauma team told me later that the anatomy of my throat made it difficult to allow intubation (placing of a tube down my throat to send oxygen through to my lungs). The staff tried seven times before successfully intubating me. He told me that for four hours he "air-bagged" me, "not a good source of oxygen for the human body," he said. Also, I learned later that EMTs had tried twice to intubate me prior to the trip to the hospital. Intubation, I heard later, is itself a risky procedure.

Our daughter Rebecca was certainly having a twenty-third birthday with more excitement than we had planned. She and her boyfriend Nate arrived at the hospital first. Since no identification had been sent with me, I was a Jane Doe. When Rebecca inquired about my whereabouts, personnel could not answer her without a name and they couldn't locate any information. Thinking I had not yet arrived, she and Nate decided that they would leave the hospital and walk around outside a little. After getting some fresh air they walked back in and again asked about me, hoping someone could track me down by that time. Suddenly something occurred to Nate, who has a keen memory. He had noticed what I had been wearing while mowing the grass earlier and he gave the desk personnel a description of my outfit. That rang a bell and they did determine I had been brought in already, but to no avail. They were told my condition was very poor, and they weren't allowed to come in to see me. They took that as very bad news.

Meanwhile, the rest of my family began arriving. In addition to my husband and my two sons, two of my brothers and their wives arrived. Around the same time my eighty-five-year-old dad Garland and his sister Betty came into the room, followed shortly after by my pastor Ed Heatwole and his wife Eileen. Two other pastors from our community also came when they received the news.

They were all directed into the family room away from the busy waiting room. Our pastor's wife aptly named it the "Bad News Room." She explained later that this area is generally where families are given the bad news about their loved ones.

And bad news is what it seemed they were getting. Doctors began filing into the room telling my family that there was not a lot of hope to be given. Carlton said later he remembered that most of the people there felt pretty hopeless about my pulling through. One doctor commented that on a scale of one to ten, with ten as the worst, I was above ten.

The doctors explained that during the cardiogenic shock, since my lungs were filled with blood and fluid, I wasn't getting oxygen. If I did make it, I would more than likely be "brain dead." The doctors planned to order neurological testing to see what damage had already occurred.

The doctors continued to come into the room, bringing despairing news. "We really don't know what to do; we are taking a shotgun approach," they told my family. "We have about fifteen staff members working over her." Time after time, they came in with announcements that held little hope. How much worse could it get? Each wondered.

My father's pastor, Barbara, had arrived at the hospital and she quickly went over to him. She knew my father and his family well, having stood with Dad in times of grief several times before. She placed her hand gently on his arm and offered her comfort. He was shaking. As he sat there trembling, he prayed, "God, please, no! Spare me from losing another child!" He quietly cried and pleaded with God.

My dad was no stranger to grief and loss. Forty years earlier, he and my mother had had to kiss a stillborn daughter good-bye and bury her. Born after Carlton, she would have been my little sister. Twenty years after that he said goodbye to his mate of forty-three years, my mother. A few years after losing my mom, my dad became reacquainted with a girlfriend he had dated many years before, prior to my mother. She lived in Colorado, so after a few years of a long distance relationship, they decided to marry. It was good to see my dad happy again. And then after only five years of marriage to Dad, his wife June died of amyloidosis, a potentially fatal condition in which abnormal proteins build up in a person's organs. We stood and watched with sadness as our dad buried another mate. But that wasn't the last time he would lose a loved one—Mark died unexpectedly six years after that and he once again buried a child.

"Please God, no!" He continued to beg. My family sat there with him, each enveloped in his own grief and pleading.

My pastor stood up and said, "Let's all join hands and pray." Now Pastor Ed has a way of praying. Heaven just seems to open up when he prays. There is such a close and personal communication that occurs when he lifts prayers to our heavenly Father.

He started with, "God, your daughter, Teresa, is in trouble and she needs you." He continued to ask God to spare my life and to give my family comfort.

Each of my children and my husband told me later they had a peace about everything then. Amazing what prayer can do!

Five to ten minutes after they prayed, one of the doctors came walking into the room, shaking his head. Imagine the sinking feelings in my family's stomachs as he sat down! He lifted his head and announced, "This is what every doctor lives for. She's turning the corner."

"What?" everyone said. Smiles appeared. He turned to my husband and asked if he wanted to come in to see me then. Eric jumped to his daddy's side.

They walked into the room, not knowing what to expect. My son told me later he didn't even recognize me because I was so blue and swollen. When Ronnie walked over to me, he asked me a question, and I gave him a thumbs-up. Tears rolled down their faces. Later one of the doctors explained to me how moments before, they had asked me if I could hear them—if so, would I squeeze his finger, and squeeze it I did.

My husband had to laugh. "You didn't know she was a dairy farmer, did you?!" The bleak hours were appearing brighter.

What no one knew at that time was why I had squeezed the doctor's finger so hard. There was a reason—and I would tell them when I could.

Jared and Rebecca were then allowed to come in. They told me my eyes opened widely when I heard their voices. I so vaguely remember those first few moments. In a little while, my elderly dad came in and told me, "Teresa, it's Dad." I squeezed his hand. I could not talk to anyone. I was still intubated. But I had to talk! I had to tell them what I had just seen!

Emergency Medical Team Report

Prepared by Kitty Pitsenbarger

On April 10, 2006, Mt. Solon Volunteer Fire and Rescue was dispatched for an unresponsive breathing patient. When Medic 218 responded, the dispatcher advised the crew the caller stated the patient was an unresponsive 48-year-old female possibly cardiac related. While enroute to the scene we received an additional update: CPR was in progress. Firefighters were on the scene one minute later, advising a working code blue; Medic 218 had an additional 5 minute arrival on scene. Firefighter-EMT on scene requested availability of Air Care 5.

Medic 218 arrived to find patient on ground beside her residence, ashen gray with CPR in progress. Husband stated they were walking up from barn located at the base of hill; patient leaned against post to rest. Husband states he walked on approximately 20 feet and turned around to find patient on ground. The cardiac monitor was applied; patient was in v-fib. Patient was shocked at 150J by medic. Patient then went into PEA, CPR was resumed. Medic was in the process of attempting to pace, EMT-E was attempting to intubate patient and establish IV access. Firefighter-EMT was ventilating patient. An additional EMT and Firefighter on scene were also helping father equipment and assisting with patient care. Driver of 218 was setting up LZ for Air Care 5 in a pasture field directly behind patient's home. An engine company from Bridgewater responded to assist with LZ. . .

Just prior to pacing patient, patient's rhythm changed to v-tach pulseless. The patient was shocked at 150J by medic, a pulse was regained, and 1mg Lidocaine was given to the patient by medic over 2 minutes. In the meantime Air Care 5 was circling above . . .

The EMT-E and medic on the crew were unable to intubate patient. Patient had an intermittent gag reflex. A nasal airway was placed in the patient's left nare [nasal passage]. Firefighter-EMT continued to ventilate patient with BVM. Patient's color did improve.

Patient became flushed and diaphoretic [perspiring profusely]. IVs were established with 18 gauge in the left anticubital and a 20 gauge in the left hand. At this point there was difficulty keeping IVs secured secondary to the patient being diaphoretic.

Patient was being prepared for transport. Upon rolling patient onto backboard, patient returned to pulseless v-tach. Patient was again shocked at 150J. Pulse was regained. Patient remained unresponsive. Her heart rate was 147. IV fluids were open. Her blood pressure was 148/94.

At this time the helicopter crew was on the ground approaching the scene. The IV in the left anticubital infiltrated after the third shock. Patient care was then released to Air Care Medics. Patient was sedated for difficult intubation with gumbugi with Air Care Medics. An additional IV was placed in right anticubital by Bridgewater Engine Medic. Once Air Care 5 was ready, crew assisted patient to helicopter.

The patient's family did keep the crew informed of patient progress. Patient's husband reported UVA doctors did not know what kind of prognoses to give him for his wife's condition because what had happened to this patient just does not happen. Patient's husband stated there was concern for patient's heart, lungs, and neurological condition upon patient's recovery.

On Wednesday April 12, patient's husband called to give an update. Patient was doing well. She had been extubated. She was walking in her room at UVA, neurologically intact.

Patient was discharged from UVA after receiving internal defibrillator on Tuesday April 18.

Since then the patient has met with the crew who assisted with her call on April 10, 2006.

CREW	NOTES
Jeremy Kirakofe	Firefighter-EMT, first to arrive on scene
Roger Kirakofe	Firefighter-EMT, first to arrive on scene
Sherwin Campbell	Firefighter-EMT, driver for 218 on call
Bill Smiley	Firefighter, EMT-1, Crew 218
Kitty Pitsenbarger	EMT-E, Crew 218
CJ Hartman	EMT, Crew 218
Lon Dearing	Firefighter–EMT-E, Bridgewater Engine 109
Mike Peak	Firefighter–EMT-1, Bridgewater Engine 109
Travis Caricofe	Air Care 5
Betsy Smith	Air Care 5
TIMETABLE	
1329	Call received
1330	Call dispatched
1338	EMS responding
1340	CPR by family*
1341	Firefighters on scene administering CPR
1347	EMS on scene
1348	1st shock
1352	2nd shock
1358	3rd shock
1405	Air Care 5 on location
1434	Air Care 5 departed to UVA
1441	218 to RMH out of service

*Husband started CPR soon after initial call was made.

This report is reproduced in the CSEMS Council 2006 Regional EMS Awards brochure, available at csems.vaems. org/awards/2006/award_profiles.pdf. The crew on this call received an award for Outstanding EMS Call.

Answered Prayers

I can remember what happened like it was yesterday. That memory will never leave me. I saw Teresa leaning on the hitching rail and turned away for a minute, and a minute later I turned around again and she was on the ground and our dog was licking her on the face. Teresa is an animal lover, but she never lets animals lick her face—she draws the line at that! I went over to her and she was kind of moaning so I knew she wasn't dead but there was a blank look in her eyes and she didn't see me. There were some funny sounds coming from her throat—I can't exactly describe them, but she wasn't conscious. I knew it was her heart that had given out. I didn't know how to do CPR, but I remembered watching a CPR demonstration once when I was in high school. Plus, I had seen enough CPR done on TV shows that I started doing it like I had seen them do. It's a good idea for schools to teach their children and their teachers how to do CPR, now that I think about it.

—Ronnie Simmons

After I began stabilizing, the doctors felt it was safe to move me to a critical care room and out of the emergency room. I had been heavily medicated and gone through a lot of trauma, so my family felt I needed rest. One by one, they said their goodbyes and began their one hour trip back across the Blue Ridge Mountains, feeling much more positive this time than when they had come across earlier.

Once home, my husband climbed into an empty bed. He had lots to think about. He breathed up a prayer to God, asking that everyone would get a restful sleep. Tomorrow would come quickly. As each of my grown children went to sleep, they had the same sense of peace God had given them earlier that night. Everyone slept well.

At 7:30 the next morning, Ronnie called the hospital to check on my condition. The nurses assured him I was improving. He knew he had to do farm chores first before making the trek back across the mountain, so he and the children divided the chores and they worked quickly. Around mid-morning, driving separately, they arrived back at the University of Virginia Hospital.

As they arrived, the nurses gave instructions that only one person could come in at a time until my condition improved. (Funny to think about it now, but at times, I remember counting five or six doctors or medical staff standing around my bed at one time! Oh well, they helped keep me alive.)

I was groggy and heavy-eyed. When my husband leaned over me, I reached up and rubbed his face with my hands and knew instantly it was Ronnie. Poor thing, he hasn't even had time to shave, I thought. I felt tears on his cheeks. I wanted so badly to talk, to tell him, "I love you, I am all right," but the intubation tube would not allow me. He kissed me before he left the room, and then each of my children came in. My eyelids wouldn't stay open, but I again reached up and touched each of their precious faces. I knew them just by feeling them. Oh, children, I've got to tell you what I saw, I kept thinking.

Someone announced to me that my eldest brother, Reggie, from Charlotte, North Carolina, had arrived. Reggie had always been the strong one, the pillar, after my dad. And yet, I remembered how the tears had streamed down his face at Mark's funeral just a year and a half earlier. I realized how hard this new near loss would have hit my dad and my brothers. Reggie, this is just too fresh for your still fragile emotions, I thought. We hugged and cried together. My big brother stood sobbing, his tears mixing with mine.

My medicated state began to subside as other family members came in to see me one by one. An observant nurse noticed how hard I was trying to communicate and she ran to get me a legal pad to write on. The first thing I wrote was one word: "Why?" I was becoming coherent enough to wonder how such a dangerous situation could have happened. I had taken such good care of my body, especially after my mother had died. I had secretly vowed I would never have what she did, and so I began running three to four miles five days a week until my joints began hurting around age forty, and then I began walking on a treadmill.

No one had the answer to my question, but they assured me that I would soon be able to talk with a doctor about what had happened. I continued to "talk" with each of my visitors on the legal pad as they came into the room. I wrote a note to my next oldest brother, Randy, asking him to be sure to tell the doctors of his heart own condition. A few years prior to Mark's death, Randy's heart had been racing and leaving him short of breath. He finally went to his doctor about it. He recommended that Randy be seen by a cardiologist. After wearing a twenty-four hour heart monitor, it was discovered that Randy's heart was going into ventricular tachycardia. He was put on medicine for it, but after a few years, Randy was tired of the fatigue the medicine caused and stopped taking it. This had concerned us all. So here I was, his little sister, lying on my hospital bed and writing frantically to him, urging him to get back on his medicine so that he would not end up in a state like me. He assured me he would.

By this point, the medical staff was allowing more than one person in the room at a time, so my younger brother Carlton and his wife Kathy came in. Carlton has always been the quiet one of the family. He was probably more typical of the middle child, always quietly standing back and observing, somewhat introverted. Seeing Carlton's and Kathy's tear-stained faces and knowing how busy they are with the duties of their farm in addition to raising three young girls moved me very much. I knew they didn't have many hours to hang around a hospital so I wrote a good-bye to them on my pad and hugged them both. They assured me they would be back the next day.

Next my dear old dad came in. Even with the solid build my dad possesses, he looked so frail. I wondered if he had had any sleep. He had to be tired. When he reached down to hug me and our faces met, I felt the wetness from his tears. How many tears had he wept in his lifetime? He had experienced so much sorrow. As we hugged and our tears mingled, I had to wonder what he was thinking. I am often told I look a lot like my mother. Did God do that, knowing He would be calling our mother away from us early in life? I knew my dad was feeling such a sense of relief knowing that God had heard everyone's prayers. I didn't write anything to my dad. We just hugged and cried together.

In a little while, Ronnie came back in with the doctors and my dad said he'd wait outside. I began writing notes to the doctors, asking them if they had checked things such as my free T3 levels. I wrote down a medication I had been taking. Called Armour, it is desiccated pig thyroid medication and is a natural yet patented prescription sometimes used for hypothyroidism. I wondered if I was on too high a dosage and I asked them if it was ventricular fibrillation or atrial fibrillation that had caused this trauma.

One of the doctors pulled my husband aside and asked him, "Who *is* this lady? She's asking us things we need to think about."

Ronnie laughed, knowing that just the day before, the doctors had been ready to order neurological testing on me to assess the extent of the brain damage. Now here I was, "picking their brains" with questions regarding how this had happened!

They explained to me that at sometime during my heavy medicated state they had done an echocardiogram on my heart. My heart was showing an ejection fraction of only fifteen percent, which was very severe. It had gone into ventricular fibrillation, but they needed to do more testing to discover why. The first test they wanted to do was a catheterization to see if there was any blockage.

I frantically wrote, "This is what doctors were doing when my mother had her first heart attack! Isn't there anything else you can do?"

They agreed that sometimes the procedure is risky, but to reveal answers for my condition, it would be necessary. I reluctantly agreed. They told me I could wait a few days. I remember many times during that day seeing doctors and medical staff standing and conferring around my bed, reading charts. I was told later I had defied every textbook explanation. They just could not figure out what had caused me to turn the corner!

One of the doctors reiterated to me how valuable and instrumental my husband had been in saving my life. The doctor realized that the fact that Ronnie had continued with CPR for as long as he had and with the intensity that he did was what had kept life sustained in me.

My widowed sister-in-law, Dana, was sitting by my bedside at that moment and she quietly got up and walked out of the room. I immediately sensed her hurt. She must have thought back to the year-and-a-half prior, when she had fought to save Mark's life. Sadly, on that day the EMTs were too far away. Why him and not me? That is a question I plan to ask God someday!

My husband came back into the room. It was the first time we were alone. I motioned for my pad. "I have to write to tell you what I have seen," I wrote.

Who I Saw

Teresa started writing her story on a pad for me before she could even talk. I know Teresa and she isn't the kind of person to make up something. Plus, what she told me about was so involved, there was so much to it, that I believed her.
—Ronnie Simmons

I did not yet have the strength to go into detail, especially on paper, but I had to begin telling him. Even after all those doctors had announced their astonishment at my pulling back from death's door with no apparent brain damage, I was still not as impressed with that fact as I was with another one: While my heart was not pumping I had witnessed some things that I had to share.

My husband gave me my writing pad. In big letters I wrote, "I saw Mom and Mark. There was a bright light all around them." Ronnie looked at me with tear-rimmed eyes. I wanted so badly to talk and tell him more!

He must have gone out and told my children what I had written because our oldest son, Eric, and his fiancée entered with a questioning look on their faces. I wrote to them, "I saw many people who had just died." Oh, how I needed to explain to them what I meant!

They left and got Jared and Rebecca. Jared asked me, "Mom, how bad was it?"

I thought immediately of the second place God had allowed me to see. I wrote, "Jared, it was so so so bad." I could tell by the expression on his face that he did not know what I meant.

At some point later, Rebecca and Nate came back into my room. She asked me about seeing my mother and Mark. I wrote to her, "They were so beautiful."

But there was something else I wanted her to know. I couldn't wait to explain. I boldly printed, "Rebecca and Nate, get your lives right with God!" Their eyes grew big with questions.

The day passed into the afternoon as doctors and nurses came in regularly to check on me. I dozed on and off throughout the day. When I would awaken, the big questions of why this had happened still lingered. The doctors were just as puzzled. They told me they wanted to do an MRI that night. Maybe that could give a better understanding of what was going on in my heart. I nodded in agreement.

As afternoon turned into evening, my husband and children knew it was time to leave. They needed to get back to the farm to do evening chores. Once again, we hugged and they said their goodbyes. I wrote on my pad to them, "Be careful crossing the mountain." One by one, they walked out of my room, looking back one more time as though they were reluctant to leave.

I felt a new kind of sadness at seeing them going back home. This was such a first for me. It seemed odd to be the one in the hospital room. I just never had expected a life-threatening event to happen to me at such a young age—who would have? As I listened to one after another doctor explain my condition, I could tell that they were as surprised as I was.

A team came into my room shortly after my family left and announced that they wanted to remove the tube. They felt by now that I was breathing well on my own. They must have medicated me because I don't remember their removing it. I do remember one of the doctors coming in and explaining that he wanted to remove a "pic [or PICC, for *percutaneously inserted central catheter*] line." He explained it was inserted down into my heart from my neck. To this day my skin pigmentation is changed around the site where this line was installed. People often ask questions about it.

Shortly after removal of the tube, I began coughing continuously. Even now that I could talk, the cough made it quite difficult to speak. One of the cardiologists told me that because a combination of acid contents from my stomach was aspirated into my lungs and my throat was irritated from the intubation, a severe cough would probably be around a while. And "a while" it was; that chronic cough lasted for six months, often waking me up at night.

I remember looking at the clock in my room—the time was 11:30 p.m. I wondered what my family was doing. One of the nurses came in and told me it was time to take me to have the MRI done. She and a medical transportation assistant got me over onto another stretcher and wheeled me out of my room and off to radiology.

They somehow got me into the MRI device, but I was coughing so intensely that it was hard to respond to any question they asked. The technician asked me to lie as still as I could. This was so difficult! I just couldn't suppress my cough. At some point, the technician leaned over the tube and explained they only had a few more minutes of pictures. Could I please hold still? I tried with all my might. My efforts must have been enough, because after a little while they took me back to my room.

After getting settled back into my hospital bed, the attending nurse asked if I felt like drinking anything. Did I! I felt as though I was dying of thirst. How good a ginger ale would taste! I think I must have drunk a liter of ginger ale that night. It was so soothing to my throat!

It's funny how habits continue from childhood. Often when we would get sick as children, our mother would offer us ginger ale. I've always wanted it, since then, whenever

I've been sick. This night was no exception. For the next month or so, I craved this drink. Maybe it was some kind of a connection with what our mother had done for us when we were little in order to get us well. Even repeating it today just seems so healing. Or maybe sipping it reminded me that nearly twenty years after she had passed away, I had been taken to a place where I had seen her, and I knew beyond a shadow of a doubt that I'd see her again.

My Mother, My Friend

Such blessings I have had in my life... One of my most memorable was my gentle and kind mother, Anna Belle Hite Simmons. (That's right, Simmons—I have carried the same last name all my life—though Ronnie and I are not related by blood.) My mother had to wait twelve years after marriage to my dad to experience the joy of giving birth to her first child, my brother Reggie.

She and Dad wanted children badly after he returned home from WWII. She *loved* children. She would invite nieces and nephews to stay with her and my dad on the farm during the summer months and weekends, fulfilling her desire to be a mother, but she wanted a child of her own. After a doctor encouraged them to "get away" for a little, they took a trip and shortly afterwards, Mom discovered she was pregnant. Reggie was born when she was thirty-four, and she had five more children–Randy, me, and Carlton, and then after that she had the baby girl who would have been my only sister had she lived. Last came Mark. She was forty-two when Mark was born—the same age he was when he died.

Mom was a city girl who became a farm girl when she married Dad. She hand-milked the cow twice a day, raised chickens for fresh eggs and meat, grew a gigantic garden, and canned and preserved its bounty. Dad built her a greenhouse where she spent many hours, and it was a favorite place for me to do my homework. The smells of dirt and vegetable plants still evoke many fond memories. Both she and dad were children of the Depression. They taught us early on to be frugal in our lifestyle: to save, reuse, and make from scratch when we could.

As a teenager, I sometimes heard Mom commenting that her heart "just didn't feel quite right." She wasn't a complainer so a lot more went on than we ever knew. We learned later from her doctors that she let her heart go way beyond what she should have by not paying attention to her symptoms. But that was her way, never wanting to bother anyone or complain.

After Dad retired as a postal worker and part-time farmer, he and Mom spent their winters on the Texas/Mexico border doing mission work. Mom missed her grandbabies terribly. She would hold the little Mexican babies and think of her own grandchildren.

In March of '85, Dad checked her into a hospital in Texas because a cough had held on for some time. Mom and Dad thought she had pneumonia, but the doctors knew it was something else. Mom had congestive heart failure and fluid was in her lungs. They ordered a catheterization to check for blockage in her arteries. While Dad sat in the waiting room, he heard "Code Blue" announced over the intercom. He thought, "I sure hope that isn't Belle."

It was. She was resuscitated and that is when it was discovered how bad her heart really was. All of my brothers, my husband, and I bought tickets and flew to Texas. I walked into her room. Her eyes were puffy, and I was shocked at how bad she looked.

As I bent down to hug her, she whispered something in my ear. Something she would never talk about again. She simply said, "Teresa, I saw many people who have already died when I was out." I'll never know what she meant because she never wanted to talk about it after that. I was the only one she told that to.

She didn't have a good prognosis. She had a heart arrhythmia, an enlarged heart, and congestive heart failure. They gave her eighteen months at the most. She was flown by air ambulance to MCV-Richmond as Ronnie, Mark and I drove their van back to Virginia and my other brothers flew back home. Doctors were puzzled about what to do for her. Many heart medicines were in their infancy then. The doctors tried many different kinds of them, but nothing worked.

Slowly we saw her health worsen. The summer before she died, I realized how much her condition had deteriorated, but I didn't want to accept it. On a visit to my house one afternoon, as she sat and rocked my children, she called me over to see something. Her heart was beating wildly and we could view it just looking at her blouse. Tears rolled slowly down her cheeks.

She looked up with her big blue eyes and said, "Teresa, I am ready to go on, but I'm not ready to leave you all or the grandchildren." It's a sad memory because it was at that time I had to accept the fact she would be leaving us and I think she had known how I was trying to put the thought out of my mind.

It wasn't long after that. Out of desperation, Mom and Dad asked if she could have a biopsy done in Richmond. Within a few days after Mom was admitted, she had a massive heart attack. Dad once again called us to her hospital bedside. The nurses explained some of what we could expect, but I still don't think we were prepared.

Mom was intubated and her eyes were wide open. She searched our faces as though she was trying to figure out who we were. My mom had enough pride about her that she would never have wanted to be like that. I stayed with my dad the whole time while my brothers, who had to keep up their job responsibilities, traveled back and forth.

On Friday, September 12, 1986, I left briefly to buy some groceries for my family's empty cupboards and do a couple quick loads of laundry. I arrived back at the hospital at 5:50 pm. My dad was standing outside CCU with tears welled up in his eyes. I knew immediately.

He announced, "She's gone." The nurses allowed us to come back in one last time to say our goodbyes. Mom died at sixty-six years of age, exactly eighteen months after the doctor's prognosis.

Mark and I decided to go with Dad to the little mountain cabin where he and Mom made their home so we could spare him being alone. As we opened up the door, the feeling overtook us. This was the same cabin we'd come to often as a family on weekends as children, and for the last few years it had become the year-round home of Mom and Dad. It was very difficult walking through that door knowing Mom was never going to be there again. We had to choke back the tears.

Dad continued living in the mountains and went to Texas during the winter months to help at the mission. I think it helped fill the void.

Meanwhile I felt as though my best friend had just died. In addition, the dairy was completely consuming my husband's time. I felt alone much of the time even though I had the children.

I learned to turn to God. I often thought of "Footprints." There are two or three versions of this poem, and here's one of them. Perhaps, you, too, have read it:

Footprints in the Sand

One night I dreamed I was walking along the beach with the Lord.
Many scenes from my life flashed across the sky.
In each scene I noticed footprints in the sand.
Sometimes there were two sets of footprints,
other times there were one set of footprints.

This bothered me because I noticed
that during the low periods of my life,
when I was suffering from
anguish, sorrow or defeat,
I could see only one set of footprints.

So I said to the Lord,
"You promised me Lord,
that if I followed you,
you would walk with me always.
But I have noticed that during the most trying periods of my life
there have only been one set of footprints in the sand.
Why, when I needed you most, you have not been there for me?"

The Lord replied,
"The times when you have seen only one set of footprints in the sand,
is when I carried you."

—Mary Stevenson, also attributed to Margaret Fishback Powers and Carolyn Carty

God picked me up and carried me through. I found myself forced to turn to Him. I was in every Bible study or women's church group I could join, and I really grew in the Lord. God was enough, and He was everything, during that lonely time.

A Place of Life and a Place of Death

As I lay there in the quiet room, brought back from my own experience at death's door, I felt my mother's presence close by. I thought of what she had whispered to me as the doctors brought her back from the Code Blue in Texas years before. I, too, had seen people who had died—and she was one of them. But unlike my mom when she had returned from the brink of death, I wanted to tell everyone about what I had seen.

The only sounds nearby were the muffled taps of the nurses' rubber-soled shoes in the hallway and the beeping of the heart monitor at my bedside as I recalled where I had been and the scenes I had witnessed during the time my heart had stopped.

It was very easy to let my mind return to such a pleasant place.

I kept seeing the vivid images not only of my mother but of my brother Mark in my mind all during that quiet night. Mark, the youngest of my mother's and father's five children, only forty-two when he died just a year-and-a-half before my own brush with death—Mark, who had endured some very difficult times in his life yet held onto his faith. Mark, my little brother. He and I had been very close as children. He was both a friend and a confidante. A skilled carpenter, he had built both our unusual house and barn.

The summer before his death, we had a phone conversation I'll never forget. Mark was in the midst of some personal difficulties and stressful times. He lamented how his life seemed to be going backwards. I said to him, "But Mark, just think, someday we are going to live in the big mansion that Jesus promised He is building for us. Now won't that be better any day than any house here on this earth!" Mark had agreed. I didn't know then just how soon he'd get to see his mansion. . . .

That quiet night as I remembered Mom and Mark and how I had seen them while I was a "working code," the comfort that seeing them gave me can never be expressed. I'd close my eyes and see them again—my mother looking rested and refreshed, such a contrast with the way she had looked during her long health struggle, and Mark looking as if all cares had been lifted from him so that his face radiated joy and warmth. I returned in my mind to that place of light and life. . .

***

My mother stood slightly to my left and my brother stood slightly to my right. Both reached out toward me, their arms ready to embrace me. They were in the most beautiful place surrounded by the brightest, purest light I have ever seen. The light poured out from behind them toward me. No light on earth is as brilliant as this light was. I sensed movement and energy in the atmosphere, and the peace and love I felt as I stood there was beyond any feeling I have experienced. Their two perfectly restored bodies flashed before me.

How can I ever express the feeling? There just are no words. I've often tried to explain it later by saying, "If you could take all the love, all the joy, all the peace in the world and put it all together, it still wouldn't come close to this feeling." It just felt so complete, like the feeling we look for all of our lives on this earth and never obtain. There it was all around them, just like the light that was behind and around my mother and brother and coming out toward me. Though I could not see Him, somehow I knew Christ was right there, because I sensed His presence tremendously.

As I stood there, time seemed so different. I honestly don't know to this day how long I stood there, but it seemed like a fraction of a second. It was unlike time as we know it here on this earth.

Then, just as I started to speak and to reach for my mother and brother so I could embrace them, suddenly I was taken away.

***

To this day, God has not allowed me to remember how I transitioned from there; it just happened. I lay awake most of that night, thinking about it and then closing my eyes to focus on the image of my mother and Mark.

God had allowed me to see something else during my cardiac arrest, something very disturbing and puzzling. Where had He taken me? Why did He allow me to see what I did? I could easily tell anyone who would listen about seeing my mother and brother, but what about this other scene? I didn't fully understand it yet, but I knew there was great significance to it and that I must share it when the timing was right.

I pressed my mind to play the scene again. Suddenly, and I do mean suddenly, I was standing in front of two huge grey spirit-like beings. Looming toward me, they stretched their arms out just as I had seen Mom and Mark do. I knew immediately that they were mocking my brother and my mother. It was as if they had just watched Mom and Mark and knew exactly how they had stretched out their loving and welcoming arms toward me and they were doing an evil parody of that same gesture.

I looked below me at a road filled with a crowd of people. They were walking, some of them stumbling, in front of me, and it seemed as if someone or something was hustling them along. The scene played out like a silent movie or a pageant with action but no sound, and somehow the quietness made it all the more frightening.

I saw among them several grey spirit-like beings that were shoving them forward. They were somewhat translucent, similar in substance to a cloud or mist, and their heads were hooded in large folds that draped down toward the ground—imagine the Grim Reaper and you'll get an idea of what I am trying to describe. These beings had no faces and I knew immediately that they were evil. They continued to herd the crowds of people along.

I somehow knew the two tall beings who had mimicked my mother and brother were more powerful than those other spirit creatures. While they looked similar, they were bigger, and I understood that they held a position of authority over the smaller ones.

The crowds of people being pressed to keep moving were real. They were not ghosts or apparitions. They moved reluctantly, their faces distorted with bewilderment, fear, and shock. I crouched down on my hands and knees and crawled closer to peer into their faces better. I began to not only see their fear but to sense it, and I became very frightened myself.

Two of the people looked right at me and I felt sorrow like I've never felt before. I stood up and looked into their pleading and helpless eyes. They wanted me to do something. It was very obvious they knew I wasn't supposed to be there. One of them was an elderly man, tall and bald, the other a middle-aged woman, brunette and brown-eyed, very beautiful. I remember thinking, she's so pretty. I wanted to help each of them, but fear immobilized me.

"Where am I? I thought I was saved!" I wasn't speaking the words out loud, but as soon as I would have a thought, there would be an answer in my understanding.

Immediately an answer came to my mind, or more like a thought.

"You are saved. You are an onlooker only."

I don't know how long I stood there looking. I just remember a fear as I've never had before. At that time, the tall spirit beings turned and looked at me again. I sensed they were going to come over closer to me.

I don't remember now all that took place during that moment, but I had some kind of a conversation with the Lord. "My children, my family, my loved ones, Lord, they can never come to this horrible place!" I said.

That's all I remember of the conversation. God still hasn't revealed to me all that happened during that time, but I know that I conversed in my spirit with Him somehow and I believe someday He will reveal what we talked about.

I do remember this, though: Immediately, all my fear was replaced with a tremendous feeling of peace. I sensed Christ right beside me even in that terrible place. I knew He was there, and I knew He had been there all along, but the fear had not allowed me to know it before that moment of recognition.

It was at this moment I heard an audible voice, the only actual voice I heard during this scene: "Your work is not finished."

It was somehow a familiar voice, a voice my spirit recognized. Excitement and anticipation filled me, and I knew at once I was going to be allowed to return. I knew then that everything was going to be all right with me. Somehow then, my face turned or was turned to the right, away from the scene in front of me.

Then all at once I felt a tremendous energy start to surround me. "Energy" is the only way I can explain it. I knew intuitively it was some type of a transit. It was such a strange sensation! I also knew somehow, that we (Christ was by my side) were going through enemy territory. We moved at a phenomenal rate of speed. I remember praying words like, "Jesus, don't leave me, Jesus, stay by my side," over and over."

I don't know how long I was in that place; I don't know how long the transit from the place of hopelessness and horror back to my body took. I just remember awakening and seeing two doctors in white lab coats standing over me, and one of them asking, "If you can hear me, squeeze my finger." And I did, mightily. It was the only way I could say, "Keep me here! Don't let me go back there!"

As I came back, I knew immediately that God had let me see the very beginning of a terrible place, and the scene took place right after people arrived. It would take a little more time for me to identify specifically what the place was, but there was no question it was a place of death and doom, the opposite of the place of life I had seen first. Because the people there were so shocked at where they were, with their heads turning frantically from side to side as though they were looking for some place to escape, it was clear they were in a place where they didn't want to be. The horrified looks on their faces still come back to me. It was as though they were saying, "Why am I in this place?!"

Some time later, I learned the meaning of the Greek word *apolia*. "Perish" is used in reference to this word, as in "the ungodly will perish." The word means "the realized fact after death, that salvation could have been obtained." It also has to do with being too late to be saved from doom, or hell. How sad! Now I know these people I saw had just died. They were just then realizing that they could have accepted Christ when they were alive. They understood then and there that it was too late!

Too late! How desperate a feeling. I remember as I stood there having an understanding that went something like this:

"This is it. This is a done deal for these people. There's no turning back." I realized that it was over for them, and that they would never, ever have another chance.

The deep, deep sorrow I felt for them as I stood there watching was, I'm now sure, an expression from the heart of God. Yet I also knew their decision was one that they themselves had made. God did not put them there. That certainty has stayed with me.

There is only one way to heaven, through His Son Jesus. Those people had countless opportunities on this earth, but they didn't take one. Their choice determined where they would go.

"Too late, done deal." Those words echoed through my mind as I recalled the sad, terror-filled faces. I recalled over and over the shocked looks. I knew I didn't ever again want to feel the fear that permeated this place. It was beyond any fear I've ever experienced here on this earth, but I was certain God had allowed me to feel it so that I would have an understanding of what the lost souls experience.

Those two pleading faces. That poor old man and that beautiful woman, both with the most sorrowful look that begged, "Can you do something, can you help me?!" God sent me back with that image burned on my mind, and I knew I had to share that there is a real place for the ungodly.

***

The hours passed with that subdued yet active quietness that characterizes a hospital's night shift. I heard transport personnel kicking the levers to raise bed rails in adjacent rooms and nurses calling softly to each other in the halls. The beeping of the monitors next to me continued with a soothing regularity as I once again closed my eyes and talked to God.

"What is your purpose in all of this, God?" I asked Him. "I was so close to death, and you brought me back. You let me see something. Why?"

***

At some point during the night, when one of the nurses came in to check my vitals and give me ice water, I showed her what I had written about seeing Mom and Mark on the yellow legal pad I had been given. She smiled warmly and assured me she believed me. She wanted to know more. I explained how I had felt as I stood before them and how I had seen the immense light behind and around them.

She started to leave, patted my arm, and told me again, "I do believe you." I almost pressed the "call" button for her to come back into the room. I wanted so badly to explain the other scene, but I was afraid of what she would think of me. Besides, I had not told my family yet. I knew I had to do that as soon as I could talk.

In the Doctors' Hands and in God's Hands

I slept somewhat better that night than the previous one. Around 8:00 the next morning, my phone rang. Having different tubes hanging around me made it difficult to reach over and answer it so a nurse picked it up for me.

On the other end was our family doctor, a very sweet Christian man. He told me later that he was shocked to have even gotten me on the phone. He was fully expecting one of my family members to answer. It was a nice surprise for both of us.

How significant it seems now that our doctor is a praying one! It was what made me choose his practice. He has always been there for my family in medical crisis.

One of the biggest had been the time one of our big Holstein cows smashed into the back of Ronnie's hand, tearing the skin off of it. Doctor Marsh stepped right in. That incident happened on one of the few times I was away from the farm.

My brother Carlton and his wife had asked my dad and me to meet them at the Outer Banks in North Carolina. Plans were for us to drive down and spend a couple of nights at the beach, then come back home. It was during the school year so I did not take my children along. They would just have to stay back at the farm and do chores with their "dear ole dad."

We arrived at the Outer Banks on Thursday and enjoyed our first early spring morning at the beach. We spent a relaxing day hanging around our rented cottage. As my brother and dad talked about fishing plans for the next day, Kathy and I washed dishes and discussed what we'd be doing while the guys fished.

That is the nice thing about lazy days at the beach; work did not dictate our next move. Any plan could be changed around for something else. However, never did I expect my plans to be changed so drastically. The next day, shortly after lunch, just when the fishermen planned a trip back out and Kathy and I were going to spend an afternoon tanning, I got a phone call from home. It was my husband.

My first thought was, something must have happened because it's unusual for him to be in the house in the afternoon. I was right. Ronnie didn't seem terribly upset, but he tried calmly to tell me how he had attempted to put a halter on one of our cows to hold her while he assisted the veterinarian with a difficult birth. Somehow, while he struggled to do this, his hand got caught between her and a rail. As she moved backward, his hand was smashed and skin was peeled off. It must have been a sight!

Having a veterinarian nearby is far better than nothing. He quickly dowsed my husband's hand in antiseptic and bandaged it as best as he could with materials intended for animals. I am grateful that he was able to give attention to Ronnie's hand as quickly as he did. Barns are host to bacteria that are altogether different from those to which most people are exposed.

Jared rushed his dad to our local hospital. My husband described how he felt while the nurses had scrubbed his exposed flesh—I know they were doing it for his best interest, but ouch! They wrapped his hand, gave him an antibiotic, and instructed him to keep his hand elevated. He also had to go back the next day so that they could check it again.

Ronnie was at the farm when he called me. I assured him that I would come on home. As a concerned parent, my dad insisted that he come with me. I hated cutting his trip short, but he told me he wouldn't have it any other way.

We said our goodbyes to my brother and his wife and began our six-hour trip home. We didn't yet have cell phones, and the trip was an anxious one. My husband is often a hard person to read. He tends to "play down" some situations. This time, I couldn't tell how bad his hand was from talking to him on the phone.

"God, please help us and protect Ronnie's hand," I kept praying quietly. I knew that my dad was quietly praying, as well. We arrived home at nighttime. Of course, Ronnie's hand was still bandaged, but he appeared unexcited. I think he was relieved, too, to get out of the evening chores. Jared and Ronnie's father Bill tended to the animals that night.

The next day we made the trip to our local hospital. One of the nurses cautiously unwrapped his hand while the ER doctor looked on. As soon as the bandage came off, all of our eyes grew wide as we saw his large swollen red hand; it didn't look good at all. The doctor told my husband he thought it would be best if he called our family physician.

Our beloved Doctor Marsh walked in smiling that big grin of his. Even in a gloomy situation such as that, a Christian's confidence goes a long way. We all knew Ronnie would be in praying hands, and ultimately, in God's protective hand. There is a wonderful irony in the fact that as we prayed for the healing in my husband's hand, we had faith that our heavenly Father had His own hand cupped around us.

Our doctor and friend explained he needed to keep Ronnie overnight and that he wanted to call a surgeon to look at his hand. He said that Ronnie needed to be started on an antibiotic IV immediately. I called our children to let them know about their dad's condition and to ask if, once again, we could summon help to do farm chores.

Upon hearing the news, Rebecca wanted to come be with her father. About the time she walked in, she witnessed the doctor pressing Ronnie's red infected wound, and seeing blood and pus ooze out was more than she could take.

Rebecca turned to me and said, "Mom, I don't feel so well." She turned around, took two steps and passed out. In going down, she hit her head on the nurse's desk and immediately a goose-egg bump appeared on her forehead. The doctor and male nurse rushed from my husband's bed down to the floor to help Rebecca. It seemed like forever before she came to. As she did, she looked around very confused. We explained to her what had happened and ushered her to a hospital stretcher beside her daddy.

Now we had two patients instead of one! When we saw that Rebecca was going to be OK, our doctor laughed and said, "It's not often you get a well person to walk into a hospital, get injured, and end up on a stretcher."

We all laughed and knew things would end up all right. Rebecca had a concussion and had to stay for a few of hours with instructions not to sleep for a while. She had a friend to drive her home and keep an eye on her.

Meanwhile, Ronnie was started on an IV, and a surgeon was called. God's grace was with us again. The surgeon, Dr. Harry Kraus, was a friend who attended church with us. What a relief to know we had praying doctors! As he examined Ronnie's hand, he looked very concerned. He knew we were farmers and were exposed to different pathogens from what most people are exposed to. He drew a mark on Ronnie's hand and told us he hoped the redness and swelling would not go beyond that mark. He instructed Ronnie to keep his hand elevated and that he'd be back the next day to check on him.

I realized then that my husband had no pajamas for his overnight stay. In all the excitement, we hadn't eaten anything, either. I decided to go out and buy some pajamas and to stop at a fast food restaurant for a burger for both of us. I went back, and after eating our dinner together, I kissed him goodnight and drove home by myself. Who would have ever imagined twelve hours earlier that events would turn out like this!

I slept anxiously that night and couldn't wait to call his room the next morning. When 8:00 a.m. came, I dialed his room number. Much to my surprise, our friend and family doctor answered. He and Ronnie had already figured I would call. The doctor cheerfully told me that Ronnie's hand looked much better and that the swelling had gone down considerably. Praise God! Ronnie had to stay out of the barn for a few months after that until his hand had completely healed. Jared and I worked together doing most of the chores. What a relief when Ronnie was well enough to come back on the job!

***

And so I lay in the ICU that April morning, plastic tubes dangling in all directions, bags of saline solution and medication hanging beside the bed, the steady beep-beep of monitors keeping the medical personnel apprised of the smallest changes in my heart rhythm and blood pressure, and I remembered how our doctor had been such a lifeline to us in the past. I couldn't talk much with our doctor when he called. But I could thank God for him, and I did.

I already knew that he was a praying doctor, and I remembered the assurance we had felt with having him take care of Ronnie. And now here was that same doctor calling me in a hospital an hour away to see how I was. It meant so much to hear his voice on the phone. I knew I had praying friends all around, and some of them happened to be doctors.

The Word Begins to Travel

"Teresa, I can't wait to hear more about your experience." A dear high school friend of Ronnie's who worked at UVA had found out I was in the room where I was to be prepped for the catheterization and she had stopped in see me.

As the nurse continued getting me ready, I explained how I had felt and how wonderful and bright the light was that illuminated them and the area around them. A Christian, she nodded in understanding of what I was sharing. It was pleasant to see and talk to a familiar face. I was just appreciating life so much after being told over and over again my escape from death was truly a miracle. I decided to enjoy every conversation with everyone because I was realizing how precious life really is.

What I didn't yet know was that a young technician heard my account. "Can you tell me what you saw, Mrs. Simmons?" He was preparing to shoot the dye into my arteries. "I heard you talking about it, and I'd love to hear your description of your vision."

Whether he was just trying to put me at ease or was truly interested, I gave him a short summary of what I had seen while I was unofficially dead—all I could manage. I was unashamed, whether he was a Christian or not. He nodded and didn't say anything.

Maybe he wants to let what I told him settle, I thought. I wanted so badly to tell the rest. Yet I did wonder, who would understand? I had to tell my husband. I had to tell my children, when the time was right.

The technician explained each step of the procedure he was doing and what to expect. It wasn't nearly as bad as I had thought it would be. Thank my heavenly Father, no heart attack during the procedure.

After about an hour, I was taken back to my room in the critical care unit. I was told by the nurses that some of my family had come to see me. What a blessing to finally be able to communicate with them! Dad came in first. He told me he had heard Ronnie was still doing farm chores and would be over shortly. It was so good to see Dad again. He told me how he had heard about what I'd seen, but wanted to hear it from me.

My cough was becoming more severe by that time and it made talking very difficult. I tried to explain to him about everything just as I had seen it, in between coughing spells. A sensitive person, my dad was concerned that I was wearing myself out from trying to talk. He assured me that he would be around and when I felt better, I could tell him more. Besides, he explained that his sister, my Aunt Betty, had driven him to the hospital and that she wanted to see me. He reached down, hugged me, and after leaving, sent in my aunt.

My dad's side of the family has always been rather demonstrative. I didn't know what to do when Aunt Betty walked in to my room and gasped. How must I have looked to her? She quickly explained, "Teresa, I was expecting you to look so much worse! You look as though nothing happened to you." I was relieved at her explanation. We laughed together. She hugged me and expressed how glad she was that I had made it through.

Betty is my dad's little sister. She came along ten years after my dad's birth, so she was quite a surprise for my grandparents. She and her husband and four children lived just a short distance from our house where I grew up. She and my uncle had bought a little country store from my grandparents and operated it for years. What a treat for us kids to walk down our country road with five cents and buy a candy bar from my aunt and uncle's store! I also made many trips up and down that road to buy things for my mother when she needed an item for dinner.

My grandparents built a house right behind the store, and I would often go say hello to them before going home. It was an ideal life in the country growing up. All of our family; grandparents, aunts and uncles, lived very close to one another. I think it was because of this that my immediate family has remained so close. We find peace, comfort, and encouragement in one another.

When my uncle and aunt decided to retire, they sold the little country store to an outside party. They felt it was time to travel and enjoy life. Tragically, one day in December a few years later, my uncle died of a heart attack. My aunt was devastated. He was her high school sweetheart and lifetime mate! How could she carry on without him? It was a very sad winter for all of us as we saw her picking up the pieces of her life and trying to remain strong for her children. The same strength I had witnessed in my dad I had seen in my aunt. What a Godly heritage they possessed!

And there she was next to my bed and all the tubes and monitors, her cheery demeanor lighting up the room, never hinting of the sadness she had lived through. "I've been bringing your dad over each day, but I haven't come into your room. I thought I should wait until you were strong enough for more company," she said.

Good ole Aunt Betty, the ever thoughtful one. She told me how she had received a phone call just two days earlier from my brother Carlton. He was trying to locate my father to tell him what had happened to me.

Thank goodness, my dad is always careful to tell someone in the family if he decides to leave the house for a little while. This particular day, he had told my aunt he was going up into the mountains to check on things at his cabin. Not wanting to call and announce to my dad over the phone, my aunt decided personally to drive to the cabin, get my father, and tell him. And that is what she did. She also proceeded to drive him to UVA.

Every family needs someone in the family like Aunt Betty! She hugged me and told me, "I don't want to wear you out, you need your rest." She left the room with the assurance that she was praying for me and would continue.

I dozed most of the morning when the coughing spells would allow. Shortly after lunch, my brother Carlton and Kathy came into my room carrying flowers. Kathy is such a giving person. I think she brought something with her during each visit. Because of my cough, I was limited as to how much I could talk, but it was good to see them. They told me they couldn't stay too long; they had to be home before their girls got off the school bus, but how they just wanted to see me. They had talked to my other brother Randy earlier, and because his job was some distance away, he wouldn't be able to come see me. I understood they needed to get on with their lives. Knowing how busy they were, it still impresses me to this day how much they all came to see me during my eight-day stay. Carlton and Kathy said their good-byes with a promise that they would be back.

"Sorry I'm so late." Next to appear in my doorway was my beloved husband. He bent over and kissed me. He looked so tired. Dairy work is a very demanding occupation. We have always been the primary operators with help from our family members. Ronnie owed me no excuses. I knew full well he was trying to get work done so that he could come as soon as possible.

"How much rest have you been able to get?" I choked out between coughing spasms.

"Enough," he answered—though I doubted he had had much. He told me our children would be coming to see me as their jobs allowed.

"Teresa, you have a lot of admirers," he said with a smile, pointing to the arrangements that were already lining my windowsill. "I'm sorry I haven't had time yet to buy you anything." He hung his head and I squeezed his hand. Imagine that! The man who had done CPR on me successfully and kept me alive until the EMTs arrived was apologizing for not buying me flowers! I have often wondered since what token of appreciation can one ever give to someone who has saved a life?! To assist in saving a life is one of the greatest gifts ever!

Ronnie asked how I was feeling and I assured him that I was doing better by the hour. The day before, our daughter had brought a guest book to my room for guests to sign. As Ronnie looked through it, it was apparent I had had guests and must have been asleep when they came. There were signatures by family and friends, and I wasn't even awake to visit with them. How badly I felt thinking some of these people had driven over an hour to come see me just to find me asleep. They explained to me later that they fully understood why I didn't acknowledge them after the tragedy I had just been through.

"The EMTs who were on call on Monday have been calling me to learn how you're doing," Ronnie said.

"They have?"

"You had a very close call," Ronnie answered. "Kitty just told me she thinks you need a defibrillator inserted in your chest."

Neither of us at the time even knew what a defibrillator was. Imagine that, I thought. Me, the holistic person, carefully taking my vitamins and minerals over the years, eating wholesome foods, exercising often, having some foreign computerized device implanted into my chest?

"No way!" I told my husband. He raised his eyebrows at me.

"Teresa, she's a nurse. She's seen lots of situations where people have needed these and didn't have them and later died because of this. She said if she was the patient, she would lock herself in a room here until they put one in."

OK, now he had me thinking. The reality of how slim my chances of survival had been really hit me then. Yet I did not know what the right course should be.

Kitty's timing was ironic. Shortly after Ronnie brought up the idea of a defibrillator to me, two cardiologists came into my room. They had seen the results of my MRI and catheterization. The good news was that I had no blockage. My vessels were very clear, they told me. My heart was damaged, though. They still didn't have all the answers as to why my heart had done this, but clearly they were dealing with the electrical conductivity of the heart and not the "plumbing." They told us that they wanted to talk to us about implanting a device in my chest. A defibrillator!

Ronnie's conversation with Kitty had been very timely. The doctors explained in more detail what the defibrillator would do. Basically, they told me if my heart ever went into a lethal rhythm again, the device would shock my heart back into correct rhythm. It would be like having a rescue squad in my chest.

How could I leave the hospital without it, I thought. A life-saving device—how could I turn that down?

Later that afternoon, another cardiologist came into my room and told me he wanted to talk about medication. At that time, I felt I had turned around 180 degrees. When one is very holistic and seldom takes medication for anything, this is a bit too much. I had already written on my pad the previous day that I had used supplements and that I wanted to continue to do so. I explained again to this doctor how conservative I've been over the years with taking medicine and was still hesitant about taking it. It gave me the opportunity to reveal why I felt the way I did. I told the doctor that twenty years prior I had witnessed my mother having to take handfuls of medicine that her doctor had prescribed. She would tell us how badly she often felt after taking them. It seemed every time she went back to the doctor, she was given another prescription to try. She did this for eighteen months, only to get worse as the months passed.

What I didn't realize until the cardiologist explained it was that medicines for irregular heart beats were in their infancy then. Treating the condition was a relatively new science that still was not understood and the array of medications available for cardiologists to prescribe today were barely surfacing then. He said, unfortunately, a lot of medicines then were trial and error.

"I have confidence in our medications today and I've seen improvements in irregular heartbeats in patients who have taken them," he reassured me.

I had to turn all information over in my mind for a little while. I hesitantly nodded and asked, "Can we approach this as conservatively as possible?"

He agreed and said there were two medications he definitely wanted me to use—a beta blocker, which controls cardiac arrhythmias so the heart can relax after an attack, and an ACE inhibitor, which helps blood vessels to enlarge or dilate so that my blood pressure would be reduced.

My endless questions must surely have annoyed him, I thought. But he never showed any signs of it. He always took the time to answer my questions. He's a gem, and he remains my cardiologist to this day.

The doctor dismissed himself and left us some time to think about these new changes in our lives.

That's Why You're Back Here with Us

For some reason, the whole time Teresa was there I never felt like she was going to die. After the EMT put her in the helicopter he told me that there was a 50% chance or more she would die. For some reason I had a peace about me. I cannot explain it, I don't know why, but we went on over to the hospital. Everyone there seemed like they thought it was the end, but I never felt that. I just had a peace that she would pull through.

—Ronnie Simmons

The cardiac unit waiting area must have had quite a crowd in it with all the people coming and going: my brothers, my sisters-in-law, our children and their children, my dad, and pastors who knew our family and came to pray with us, and friends. I guess the nurses thought my condition was improving because they were letting more members of my family into the room. Everyone respected my need to rest, though, and I slept until dinner.

After eating my meal, the attending nurse told me that my family was still around and wanted to see me. First my dad came in to tell me he had been there all day, hanging out with Aunt Betty. He only stayed a short time with me, saying he wanted me to get my rest but promising he'd be back the next day.

Jared's girlfriend, Whitney, had been in Texas on a work-related meeting. She had just gotten back and she came into my room with Jared, her face lit up with a big smile. What a joy to see her. Her eyes were rimmed with tears. She is such a compassionate person. Her close friend, Clayton, came in after a bit. What special friends my children have, I thought.

Eric and his fiancée Rachel were not too far behind, and then Rebecca and her boyfriend Nate appeared. We talked some about what the doctors had discovered and the procedures they wanted to take. The kids assured me that things were being taken care of at home. Loving neighbors and friends had been bringing in food.

"And Mom, don't worry about the housekeeping," one of the kids said. "We're on top of it." They were even ironing clothes for their dad to wear to the hospital, they told me. How comforting to know my family could take matters into their own hands and be proficient.

After a bit, they said that they had better leave and get back to the farm chores, and Ronnie came in to say his goodbye. Now that we were alone I felt free to tell him a little bit more of what I'd seen while I was "out." Where could I start? I knew he needed to go home, but this was the first opportunity I'd had alone with him since the tube was out.

I grabbed his arm and said, "Ronnie, I saw more. I want to tell you about it. I want you to go home soon, but let me tell you what I heard." I knew I would be safe telling him what I had witnessed. I was very guarded with whom I wanted to tell as yet.

"I don't fully understand everything I saw, but I want to tell you about it," I said. "Ronnie, I heard an audible voice. I heard, 'Your work is not finished.' With that said, I was suddenly looking up at the doctors in the emergency room."

I wanted so much to tell him the rest, but I was still playing it over and over again in my mind and trying to make sense of it. Ronnie looked at me and answered very matter-of-factly, "That's why you're back here with us, then."

That simple statement reinforced what I felt—that God had a plan. He did want me back. He wanted me to tell what

He allowed me to see that day. I just didn't know how I could go about telling it.

"Ronnie, I have more to tell you, but you need to go on home now," I said. He hesitated a little but didn't argue, and then he leaned down and kissed me goodbye. I told him just as I told the children each time, "Be careful going across the mountain."

Then I was alone once again with my thoughts, prayers, and memories—and with the growing urgency to share what I had seen. Not for the first time, nor would it be the last, I prayed, "God, what did you allow me to see?" No answer came, but a peaceful feeling settled in for some time after that.

"Your Story Gives Me Goosebumps"

I always felt a sadness to see my family walk out the door and go home without me. But I also needed the rest—I was still so, so weak. I knew it would be some time before I would have my energy back.

Later that evening, one of the nurses came to my bed and asked if I felt I could stand and move around a little. Weak as I was, I still knew I should try. She convinced me that she'd be right by me. I carefully brought my legs around as she instructed me on how to get up. Funny how all my life I'd never thought anything about jumping out of bed, getting up and walking. This time, it was a thought-out, planned process. As I brought my legs around and rose to sit up, I felt very lightheaded. The chronic cough I'd been experiencing worsened. The nurse was patient with me. I suddenly felt like a ninety-year-old woman. (Later as I walked around the cardiology section of the hospital, I realized most of the patients were considerably older than I, bringing home the fact how rare heart diseases occur in younger ages.) Finally, the moment my feet touched the floor, it was time to put weight on them and stand. I felt as though I was learning how to walk all over again. I felt pressure put on my arm by the nurse who was trying to steady me. I felt so wobbly. She let me take a few minutes to gain my composure, and then asked if I wanted to take a few steps.

"Sure," I replied, biting my lip. Why did my legs feel like rubber? I wondered. After each step, I became more confident. My strength was barely trickling in, but I knew I had to do this to get stronger. She led me around the room, and by that time, I was ready to sit back down. My heart was pounding.

Thinking back now, I am amazed that I could do anything with my heart operating at only fifteen percent of its capacity. Each day, though, I felt that I could do a little more than I was able to do on the previous one.

I must have dozed off a little. I awoke to the nurse telling me it was time to move. I glanced at the clock on the wall. It was 11:30 p.m. I remembered just the night before looking at that same clock, and seeing 11:30 as they wheeled me to have my MRI done. What was it about that time? I laughingly commented to the nurse, who had been the same one to take me to radiology the night before, "Didn't we do this at the same time last night?" She laughed, too, when she realized it was the same time. I guess I did little things to make myself smile. It was just so good to be alive!

They put me into a room where I was to stay for the remainder of my time there. I slept fitfully that night because my cough allowed very little rest. The nurse came in at different times to check my vitals. The night just seemed to take forever.

The next morning I awakened to a cheery nurse. She commented on the beautiful flowers that were still accumulating. It wasn't long before breakfast came. Food was just beginning to taste good again.

Shortly after I finished my breakfast, one of the doctors came in to tell me that they hoped to schedule the surgery for the following day, Friday. My stomach tightened. I guess I just hadn't thought about it as surgery. Sensing my apprehension, he told me it was a relatively simple process and that I'd be awake throughout the procedure. That sounded better. He read over my chart, listened to my heart with his stethoscope, and asked how I was feeling. The only complaint I really had was my unending cough. He told me that pneumanitis, an inflammation of the lungs, had set in due to the acid contents that had ended up in my lungs. He told me that they had placed me on a high-powered antibiotic for it, but to expect a cough for a while. He encouraged me to try to get up and move around so that no blood clots would form in my lungs.

"Exercise would be good," he said. The doctor didn't have to convince me of that. I knew how wonderful I had felt after running several miles a day for years. Too bad my joints had not held up better. How I missed running! I made a mental note to try to get up later and move around some.

Shortly after the doctor left, my dad's pastor Barbara came into the room. She was enthusiastic about my recovery. She told me she had been part of that prayer circle the first day I was brought over.

"Isn't God good!" she exclaimed. She didn't have to convince me! I was living proof of His goodness.

I thought for a couple minutes. Should I tell her what I had seen? Would she understand? I had wanted to tell Ronnie before I shared the experience with anyone else. The positive way he had reacted to what I told him prompted me to start telling others, so maybe that was what I should do. I'd take it slowly, just sharing the fact that I had seen my mother and brother and leaving out the other details for the time being.

And share it I did—it was so consoling to share that part. I once again told my story to Barbara of how they had reached out their arms to me.

"Your story gives me goosebumps," Barbara said. I knew what she meant—I felt them as I told her, and I still feel them every time I share it with someone.

Barbara understood! She had not been pastoring my dad's church when we lost our mom, but she had been there when Mark died. This fact made my seeing him even more significant for her. She had played a vital role in counseling and comforting us during that traumatic time in our lives. We would never forget the shoulder she'd lent to cry on, nor the prayers she'd lifted for our family.

I was so glad she had come to see me. I knew that she was one of the few who happened to have a defective heart problem that was similar to mine—from time to time her heart would go into ventricular tachycardia, that fast and sometimes irregular heartbeat that my own heart had gone into before it stopped beating. She understood from personal experience the frustration we'd experienced when we questioned, "Why?!" "Why me?" "What is causing this?"

Barbara visited an hour or so, prayed with me, and then said her goodbyes. It was time to rest a little more. I needed to prepare for my big adventure of the day—walking down the hall.

I Walk, I Talk, and I Wait

"I want to try to stand up and walk," I said to my nurse.

She encouraged me to do so. Just about that moment Aunt Betty and Dad walked into my room. Perfect timing–I'd have some one to walk with! They were elated to see me standing. My dad encouraged my aunt to go ahead with me while he waited in my room. The nursed walked behind us to make sure I could ambulate around all right. Amazingly, I got as far as the nurses' station. I felt as though I'd run five miles. I stood there for a little while and asked if I could walk a little farther.

"Sure," the nurse encouraged. I got braver and walked two times that length from their station. After I stood there, I regained some strength and I walked a greater distance with my aunt by my side.

"I think I can still go farther," I told Aunt Betty.

"Are you sure you can do this?" She questioned me. I assured her, if I rested in between, I felt well enough to walk the length of that particular hallway, and that is what I did. I knew I had to rest a good bit in between, but I was ecstatic that I could go so far after just walking a few steps the night before. Not wanting to be responsible for anything happening, my aunt convinced me that I had better quickly get back into my bed. I did, but I was overjoyed over what I had just accomplished. I knew somehow I was going to recover.

After staying a little while, my aunt and dad said they would leave and find some lunch around town. My family has always associated food with anything we do together. This week would be no different. It was just as important to them at this time to eat and be together. Thankfully, I didn't have my normal appetite yet, or I would have yearned to be eating with them. They said goodbye and told me that they would be back later that afternoon.

I nodded off some. Sleep was still not coming to me—looking back, I think between the trauma I'd just been through, the new medicines I was taking, and the chronic cough, it was difficult to go into a restful sleep. It didn't take much to awaken me. I soon heard the jingling cart of lunch coming around.

The doctors had put me on a "heart healthy" diet, even though tests had come back showing my vessels clean and clear. "It was just a good practice to get into," they said. No caffeine was allowed in my diet and I missed my beloved robust coffee and southern ice tea. I knew then there would have to be some changes made, though, to improve my heart's condition.

After eating my lunch, I clicked through channels on the TV. I've never been much of a TV watcher, so it was hard to pass the time with that. I knew my husband would be coming soon and I decided I'd have him bring some books from home. Hopefully, I thought, he hadn't left. I did catch him in time. He felt as though I had sent him on a treasure hunt looking for my books. I had various ones in numerous places.

I had taken a massage therapy course a year before this happened to me and I had studied anatomy and physiology. The school explained to us that they wanted massage therapy to be recognized by the medical field, so they were gearing their courses more that way. I found anatomy and physiology to be fascinating. I knew I had a very good book on these topics and it was one I asked my husband to bring along. While I had him on the phone, I figured this would be a good opportunity to gather a gown, robe, slippers and toiletries from home. He came in later carrying a suitcase and a bag with my books, and other necessities.

"The plans are to put the defibrillator in tomorrow," I told Ronnie.

"Maybe you'll be able to come home soon after that," he said.

When one of the nurses came into my room, we asked about the procedure. She explained that I couldn't have any food or water prior to the surgery. "Oh, a killer," I thought. My unquenchable thirst right now had driven me to drink over a gallon of water a day. How could I go for very long without it?! She continued to say she really didn't know what time the procedure would take place; it would depend on how many emergencies they had ahead of me.

"Unfortunately," she followed, "if the surgery doesn't take place on Friday, we'll have to wait until Monday. They wouldn't do this on a weekend."

Bummer, I thought. This was going to be Easter weekend. How could I be in the hospital on Easter? After my mom passed away and because I have no sisters, I had always felt responsible for coordinating holiday meals for our family. Plus, my sisters-in-law were all busy with their own family plans. And what about the Easter baskets? Even though my children were grown I still loved fixing Easter baskets for them. Who could do this?

Sensing my uneasiness, the nurse followed up, "Now, I'm not saying you won't have your surgery tomorrow. We just don't know for certain." She went on to say that if I did have the procedure done on Friday, I'd be able to come home on Saturday if all went well. My husband and I were happy to hear this.

"Now, Teresa, you're not going to be doing any work on Easter this year if you get to come home," Ronnie said. I guess it was still hard for me to think realistically; my work load would have to be limited for a while. It was just hard to accept that fact.

Ronnie and I talked about various subjects that afternoon. How would we continue with the farm? What would we have to do to accommodate this heart condition? Would it drastically change our lives? So many questions, so few answers. We knew we couldn't worry about things we knew nothing about yet. God had seen us through dire situations before, and He would again.

The one subject I didn't bring up was the rest of what I had seen in the spiritual world, and Ronnie didn't, either. I was still praying to God to give me a better understanding of what He had allowed me to see. It was still a very profound occurrence above and beyond what had happened to me physically. I wasn't ready yet to tell others since I didn't understand myself the reason for God's allowing me to witness such a scene. Also, the timing and the setting for my opening up to others had to be right. Now just wasn't the time—but I grew slowly more confident that the right time would come.

...And I Wait Some More

It wasn't long before our kids arrived at various times in the afternoon. It was always so good to see them. I learned later that Eric and Rebecca had taken off the entire week from work and Jared had sent some of the horses back home that he had intended to train. Everyone was "picking up the pieces" and doing what had to be done. They told me neighbors and friends continued to bring food and to make phone calls to assure us that they were praying. I'd never been in this position where I needed so much help, but God was putting it on the hearts of people to come to our aid. I felt overwhelmed and blessed at the same time. We visited as a family there in my room until dinner. They needed once again to go home and carry on with farm chores. I asked them to lift up a prayer for surgery to go well the next day. I knew I probably wouldn't see them before that. We kissed, hugged, and said our goodbyes. With a tear running down my cheek, I watched each of them walk out the door. "God, guide them safely home," I prayed.

Dinner came around. I remember wondering if this might be my last meal for a while, since I would not get anything the next day prior to surgery. I relished every bite of the meal.

What would I do to pass the time, I wondered. I opened my Bible. How good it felt to have God's word back in my hands. The Psalms were always a comfort to read. The Bible fell open to Psalms 94:17, to be exact. It was God's word for me.

"Unless the Lord had given me help, I would soon have dwelt in the silence of death (NIV).

How much more appropriately could it be told? God's Word once again was right on. He had saved me; He had helped me; He had brought me back from the shadows of death; and He wanted to tell me that from His Word. I didn't even have to search through the Bible for it. It fell open to that exact Scripture and my eyes landed on that exact verse. Perfect! Just like God.

I turned to Psalms 23. What did David mean when he wrote about the valley of the shadow of death? What exactly had I seen? "God, where was this place I saw?" I asked once again.
The quietness of the moment brought assurance that He would answer. Somehow, I would know. I read various other comforting Scriptures. It consoled me just to read His promises. He would take care of me. I didn't have to be anxious about anything. He had told me that my work was not finished. There was more to do. My life was not to be over with. He had a plan. "God, I need to lean and depend completely on you," I prayed. I slept better that night.

***

5:00 a.m. . . . The dairy girl still hadn't left me. I was wide awake. This is the day, isn't it? I asked myself. I glanced at the erasable board on my wall where the CNA had marked the previous day. Yep, this is Friday. And then I remembered: no food, no water. A depressing thought already so early in the morning!
I turned on the TV for news. There was not much encouraging to watch. I clicked through other channels and found a Western. I wonder if Ronnie might already be awake watching his beloved Westerns, I thought. Other than riding his horses, watching old Westerns is a favorite way to spend

what little time he has for relaxation. I knew he would try to get work done first and probably wouldn't be here until after the surgery—that is, if it even happens today, I thought. I watched some of the movie and dozed off intermittently. It was hard not picking up my Styrofoam cup of ice water and drinking it.

In a little while, a nurse came in to check my vitals. I asked her if I could just chew on a little ice to relieve my dry mouth. She gave me a little with instructions to keep it limited. After that, one of the electrophysiology doctors came in. He wanted to talk to me about the surgery. What I didn't know and hadn't heard yet was that there were risks involved, even death. He wanted me to sign a consent form.

I had to agree right then and there that I understood I could die from the procedure and yet I wanted it done anyway? Tears welled up in my eyes. This was really getting to be too much for me! It was a huge decision just to go on the medicine and then another to have some foreign device implanted in my chest and corkscrewed into my heart; now they were telling me that there were risks involved. It was more than what I was ready to hear. The doctor told me if I needed a little time to think things over, he would give me time. I bit my lip and nodded.

As soon as he walked out of the room, I dialed our home phone number. I hoped Ronnie would still be in, and fortunately, he was. I tearfully told him what the doctor had just said. He knew how upset I was anyway with all the radical changes. He tried to calm me and finished by saying that he would call our Pastor Ed for prayer. I felt better and told him I'd call back if there was anything else I felt he should know.

In a few moments, my phone rang. It was Pastor Ed. How good it was to hear from him! "Ronnie just called and told me about the fears you're feeling," he said. "Would you like for me to pray with you right now?"

"You bet," I responded. Ed could move mountains with his prayers. My emotions went from extreme fear to a gentle peace immediately after praying over the phone with him.

Pastor Ed finished the conversation by reminding me what Ronnie had shared with him. "God told you, 'Your work is not finished.' You need to remember that. He is not going to bring you back only to take you away again." What reassuring words! God had put just the right words in his mouth, and I needed to hear them.

Sure enough, the doctor walked back into my room. He found me much more confident than I had been. I told him I was ready to sign the consent form. After I did, he told me that they had not lost a patient yet doing this procedure. I think he was half joking, but it was good to hear, anyway. When I asked him what time I could expect to go into surgery, he replied he really didn't know. "Friday is one of our busiest days, but will get you in as soon as possible," he answered.

I got my Bible again and started reading. I turned to Psalm 91:14:

> "'Because he loves me,' says the Lord, 'I will rescue him; I will protect him, for he acknowledges my name.'"

I flipped to another favorite passage, Psalm 46:1-2a, and then to Psalm 16:8b:

> "God is our refuge and strength, an ever present help in trouble, therefore we will not fear."
>
> "Because he is at my right hand, I will not be shaken."

What a tremendous comfort I drew from God's Word! I felt as though He was right there reaffirming those words.

Never in my life had I realized how alive God's word really is. The peace it gave me was the substance to which I held.

It wasn't long before my husband appeared in the doorway. "I wanted to come early. I thought you could use the company," he said. He told me that Eric and Rachel were milking and doing the feeding chores along with Devin so that he could come over early. He said he was actually surprised to see me still in my room because he thought I would probably already be in surgery. I had thought the same thing.

When one of the nurses came in, she told us they were still waiting to hear when they could take me. She again explained that Fridays can get very busy and that she knew there were a number of patients before me. "Don't get too disappointed if you have to wait until Monday," she finished.

That wasn't what we wanted to hear! I just wanted to get it done and go home. My husband nestled down into the vinyl chair and looked as though he was planning a nap. We found a Western channel and somewhere during the early part of the movie we both dozed off. I guess that was the best way to pass the time. It wasn't long until lunch time came.

My dad, Aunt Betty, Carlton, and Kathy showed up. They, too, were surprised that I hadn't already gone into surgery. We told them the unfortunate news of a number of patients waiting before me and that I might have to wait until Monday.

By now, the nurses didn't seem to mind large numbers of company in my room. We visited together for around an hour and they decided they would go find some lunch and come back later. Ronnie said he'd stay. We all tried to talk him into going along to get something to eat, but he insisted that he just wanted to stay and take a nap.

I guess it was then I realized how tired he must have been. I wondered if he was resting and eating properly. After my family left and one of the nurses came in to check my vitals, she mentioned something about lunch to my husband. When he told her he thought he would just stay in my room, she left for a short while, and came back with a turkey sandwich for him. Maybe it was apparent to the nurses how worn out my husband was becoming. What compassionate care! He felt bad eating in front of me, but I assured him that I really wasn't hungry, just anxious to get the procedure completed. He ate his sandwich with no more protests.

It wasn't long before my family reentered the room. They were surprised again to see me still there. We visited for a couple of hours, with everyone occasionally glancing at their watches. Around 3:00 p.m., they felt they should head home. No one had given word yet about my surgery taking place that day. It didn't look as though it was going to happen. They said their goodbyes and assured me that they would keep praying. Ronnie and I were by ourselves once again. It was good to have his company to help pass the time.

Around 4:00 in the afternoon, one of the nurses came in and announced the unwelcome news. Surgery would be put off until Monday. The doctors just simply had too many patients that day and a number of them were emergency surgeries that took longer than they had planned.

"I know you've got to be starved; I'll go get you something to eat," she said. Not really what I wanted, but by then I was getting hungry. Again, a turkey sandwich appeared. Must be what's on the menu today, I mused. I didn't take long to scarf it down, though.

"I'm thinking it would be best if I go on home to start evening chores," Ronnie suggested. He sounded as disappointed as I felt. If I'd had the surgery done that day, I could possibly be going home the next day, but it just wasn't going to happen that way.

After Ronnie left I thought about the fatigue I had seen in his face and I knew the long trek across the mountain was wearing him out. I realized that the doctors couldn't take me until they had a space, but those human emotions still bubbled up. The thought of spending Easter weekend in the hospital depressed me. I cried silently a few times. "How much longer, God?" I asked. "My family needs me."

Those sad twins named "Loneliness" and "Helplessness" might have gotten the best of me, but I soon realized God wasn't going to let me get lonely. In a little while, in walked my three nephews and my niece, Mark's children. What a joy to see them and hug them! One of their aunts had brought them to the hospital. As I looked into their faces, I could see such strong reminders that their daddy lived on. He left a little piece of himself in each one of them.

Somehow I had gotten a very distinct impression shortly after Mark's death that it would be up to us siblings and our dad to pray for the salvation of Mark's children. It was as though some kind of spiritual baton was passed on to us that day. That burden burns in the hearts of each of us. We have all admitted to each other the reality of it and we have continued to pray for them.

As they stood around my bed, I shared the fact that I had seen their dad at heaven's gates. We've often reassured them that because he had loved Jesus, he was in heaven waiting on them to join him someday. There was something very special in that moment as I told them how I had stood before him and my mom. Their eyes grew big and glistened. They knew he was there. This wasn't some "made up, feel-good" fable; they knew this was for real. They knew me. They knew I was sincere, and they already knew my love for Jesus. I told them how excited their dad was and how he had reached out to embrace me.

"One day, we will all be able to embrace him and to hug on Jesus, too!" I said. "He wants each of you to live a life just the way Jesus wants you to, so that we can be there with him." Their precious smiles were affirming their acceptance of what I had just shared. They knew.

Those children are very special, a joy to my heart. It did me so much good to be with them. They were out of school for Good Friday and wanted to spend their day on a visit to their aunt! Realizing they had given up their free time made the visit mean even more to me. Around dinner time, they felt they should leave. I kissed and hugged each of them. "You've made my day," I told them. I also thanked their aunt for bringing them.

Watching family walk out that door left me feeling lonely again, but I realized that not having surgery that day allowed me to share with those precious children how I had seen their father. God's hand was once again upon the events in my life, and in theirs. Before long Rebecca called to check up on me and she put Jared on the phone, too. They weren't going to be coming that day because they were doing chores and keeping the house in order, but their voices on the phone were a source of comfort to me.

I realized that it would probably be a long night. By now, I knew TV channels were very limited. My eyes were growing tired of reading. What would I do to pass the time? I heard the familiar clinking of the food cart coming around. Even though I had just had the turkey sandwich a few hours previously, the idea of eating dinner was appealing. The way I reasoned it, since I hadn't really eaten breakfast or lunch at the regular hours, I was okay to eat again, and it was something to do.

As I ate, I smiled a little at my relationship with eating through the years. I ate reasonably healthy, even going on some weird diets for which my family threatened to kick me out of the house. You see, I tried to get them to eat these same strange foods—if you've ever tried this, as well, you know the resistance you can run into. At the time , my children were taking packed lunches to school, so I had control over what they would eat. I would pack things like alfalfa sprouts, brown bean dip spread on blue corn chips, 100% juice, and other so-called "natural" foods. What I didn't know was that they were exchanging their lunches with other children. Imagine the joy finding out my kids were eating Ramen Noodles and Snickers bars while their peers were examining and eating hummus and other foods packed away in my kids' lunchboxes! I remember one of the kids asking me if the sprouts were what turtles ate.

It didn't take long for me to realize that my family was not happy about my ambition to feed them healthy foods. Eric expressed what they were all feeling when he came home one day, slammed his little lunchbox down on the table with tears in his eyes, and exclaimed, "I'm so tired of eating healthy—I want to eat normal food!"

I realized then I was about to turn my family away from every healthy food on the planet and send them down the junk food aisle, if I didn't let up. Through trial and error, we compromised and came up with somewhat of a reasonably healthy diet. Funny thing is that now they eat fairly healthy foods today. So I guess I didn't blow it too badly.

As I looked at the hospital food fast getting cold on my tray and the obligatory pudding dessert that I had no desire for, I had to admit something strange: The main thing different in the past few days as far as my appetite was concerned was that my sweet tooth was missing. People were already bringing Easter candy as they would come to visit, but I couldn't even enjoy it. I had always had a love for chocolate. I used to say the three basic food groups should have been changed to four: carbohydrates, protein, fat, and chocolate! I had always believed chocolate was essential in my diet—yet there the chocolate bunny sat on my nightstand, and I had no interest in eating it.

As I was commenting to one of the nurses about my change in appetite, she answered that she had seen the same thing happen in patients before. "Often after traumatic happenings," she said, "people will lose their desire to eat sweets, but unfortunately, it usually comes back." (She was right—for several weeks after I came home I had no desire for sweets. I could eat a meal and never want dessert. Sure enough, just as the nurse had said, the sweet tooth came back. Chocolate is my friend once again!)

As a farm girl lifting and doing strenuous work, I often built up quite an appetite, and so I added in a few snacks. That Good Friday evening dinner, though not large, more than satisfied my hunger. After eating it, I settled back on my bed once again and wondered what I'd do with the rest of the evening.

The phone rang. It was a distant cousin, Terry, who always cheered me up. God, once again your timing is perfect, I thought. Terry always had a positive outlook on life. He was the perfect one to talk to. Just hearing his voice and his reassurances on the phone that night settled my "down" spirits. He is one of those relatives a person just feels drawn to at family reunions because he is always fun to hang around with. He commented on my raspy voice. I explained it was from the chronic cough I had, as well as the number of intubations performed. We talked for over an hour. I told him what had happened on Monday and how I had expected to have a defibrillator implanted on this day but that the surgery had not been completed yet.

His reply was almost as if he had read my mind: "It wasn't supposed to happen today for a reason," he said. Funny how he knew to say that. As we hung up, he told me to be sure to thank my husband for what he had done.

"He saved your life, you know; you take care of him," Terry said. Even though I had heard this from a number of doctors already, somehow the point was driven home that time. Ronnie really had saved my life. That was not to be taken lightly. I continued to hold that thought as Terry said goodbye, and I thanked him for calling me. What an uplifting guy, I thought, the perpetual optimist, reminding me how blessed I am that Ronnie had been there.

When I've thought back on why I waited all day that Good Friday only to find that I had to wait some more, I am confident now that God planned it that way. First of all, I was able to encourage Mark's children. Then Terry had expressed something else that I now am confident is true: God knew something we didn't know. Maybe my heart was not strong enough yet. Whatever the reason, God knew it.

I can look back today at the disappointment we felt that day with the benefit of hindsight, but even that day, sad as I was to miss Easter at home, I knew His timing was and is perfect; He'd already demonstrated that to us. I had to rest assured that He knew what He was doing. There were too many people praying. My feeling disappointed wouldn't help anything. I had to accept things as they turned out. "There's a reason for everything," my mother used to say.

Her words came echoing back to me that evening as I laid my head back on my pillow. God's leading Ronnie to know exactly what to do still astounded me. This was my farm boy husband, the man I had taken for granted too many times. Ronnie had provided a good life for me. I was able to be a stay-at-home mom and raise our three children. He worked long, hard hours, and the results were starting to show on his run-down body. At fifty years of age, he already needed knee replacement surgery. Years prior to that, I remember years ago someone commenting that he looked like a seventy-year old man when he walked.

My thoughts went back in time, as I remembered how we had begun our lives together. . .

"Once Again, We Made It"

Our married life started with a car accident and a totaled car—on our honeymoon. As I thought about that trip, I realized once again that it had been the first time, but wouldn't be the last, that we felt God's protection on our lives.

My mind drifted back to our first date. A blind date it was—Ronnie took me to a softball game where he was playing. I remember watching him as he ran. His walk and run were unique. I often kidded him that that is what drew me to him. Ronnie was an unusual man in many ways. His love for family and animals was obvious. Not necessarily a person who is comfortable in group settings or around people, he had a love for the outdoors.

We dated for two years before getting married. We decided on a hot day in August, 1978 to bring our lives together permanently. We were two excited young people, ready to start our new lives together. After the wedding ceremony, Ronnie had planned to take me to Peoria, Illinois, for our honeymoon. He had family there who owned a farm implement dealership and thought this would be an interesting place to go visit. I was a young twenty-year-old, in love with my man, and was just happy to go wherever he wanted to take me! We often look back on his choice of a honeymoon location now and laugh. He was just being his practical self and thought nothing about the romantic side of a honeymoon. Besides, a trip to some tropical paradise would be too foreign to him.

After the wedding, we said our goodbyes to our parents and families and got in Ronnie's 1975 white Camaro, packed down and ready for the trip. We planned to spend our first night together in Wheeling, West Virginia. We were so young and naïve that we had not thought to call ahead and make reservations anywhere. We left around 5:00 p.m. and talked excitedly about our first road trip together as newlyweds. We arrived in Wheeling around 11:00 p.m. As we stopped in at the various hotels and motels, we were told no vacancies could be found anywhere. We learned that the Ohio and Indiana state fairs were going on and not to expect rooms anywhere for some distance.

Our hearts sank. This was supposed to be our honeymoon night! We looked at each other and decided to travel on and hope for the best. The route we were told to take didn't take us through many towns. We drove all night and at one point stopped at a rest stop to get a one hour nap.

We continued traveling into the early part of the next day. As the sun came up over the horizon, our eyelids were dropping heavily. We were so tired and disappointed. Somehow, we both thought marriage was just not supposed to start off this way. Little did we know what the rest of the day held!

We drove until 9:00 that morning and arrived in Indianapolis. Surely we could find a hotel now. We saw a big sign advertising a popular hotel and decided to stop. Even if we had to pay a full night's rate, it was worth it to get some rest. The hotel didn't have too many rooms, but they did have a pricey suite, we were told. We decided to take it. After resting a few hours and enjoying a buffet lunch, we figured it was time to get back on the road. We had a trip to Peoria to make.

I believe I dozed most of that day's trip. My poor husband had driven practically all night and now had to drive throughout the day. As late afternoon came, I asked if we could stop at a convenience store to get a drink. I needed to stretch a little and thought the break would do us both some good. We soon came upon a store and stopped. After we got our drink and walked around a little, we asked how far we were from Peoria.

"Not far," the store owner assured. "Maybe ten to fifteen miles." We had to laugh; we were so close and probably wouldn't have made this stop if we'd realized that.

We climbed back into the car and again continued our trip to Ronnie's cousin's house. As we were moving along, Ronnie asked if I'd get out our map so that he'd know exactly where to turn.

Just as I leaned over the console and began opening the map, I heard a startling sound. As I looked up, I saw a car coming out of a road to my right, smashing into my door that I had just been leaning against a minute before. The screaming tires and crushing metal haunted me for weeks afterward. It was a horrible image to shake.

Our car began spinning. We had just been broadsided. Our car made its way over the median strip, breaking the axle and landing in the pathway of oncoming traffic.

I began screaming, "Jesus, help us!" I suddenly recalled from my early years as a Christian being taught by Donna and her pastor that the name of Jesus had power. I had seen proof of this before but never as dramatically as then. It was just as though God's hand came down upon that car and stopped its spinning instantly.

My door was too badly smashed in to get out. I was hitting against Ronnie to get out his side. It was the only way out. Just as the car stopped, we pushed the door open and bolted out. God had prevented any other cars from hitting us. We were on the other side, just like sitting ducks. As cars came to screeching halts, people began jumping out and running to our aid. They couldn't believe that we weren't hurt and we couldn't believe it, either. Ronnie had some cuts on his face and my neck was sore, but other than being shaken up over the trauma of it all, we were OK.

We looked around to see the car that had just hit us. We saw a young boy running away, carrying a brown bag that he hid in a ditch. Other people witnessed him hiding something, as well. He was found to be quite intoxicated. When the sheriff arrived, he told us our accident was the second terrible wreck he had seen at that junction and in the first one five people had been killed. After viewing our two totaled cars, he couldn't believe that we had escaped death. However, I knew how we had. The name of Jesus had power; God had protected us.

One of the bystanders walked out to console us. We told her this was our honeymoon and that we had just gotten married. She responded with a profound statement I've never forgotten. She said, "If you can make it through this, you can make it through anything." I've often thought back on this comment, and it has proven to be true.

This accident happened before everyone carried their own cell phone. We couldn't instantly call our families back home and announce our unfortunate news. The sheriff told us that we should be seen at a local hospital and that we could make telephone calls from there. He had a rescue squad on its way shortly to transport us to the hospital. After we were seen by doctors and found to be OK, we reached a pay phone to call his cousin in order to get a ride.

He arrived a short while later. We spent our five day honeymoon beside a tranquil lake near Peoria before getting a ride back home to Virginia from Ronnie's father Bill and his uncle, who were gracious enough to drive halfway across the country and back.

***

Almost thirty years later, that event seems like a dream. I know it really happened, but because it was so distant it almost seems unreal. Time will do that; we sometimes find ourselves today pulling out old photos of our honeymoon and recapturing that moment. It's always with a feeling or statement of how fortunate we are to be alive through it all.

Lying in the hospital bed that Good Friday evening, I realized something: I was once again blessed to be alive. Ronnie was once again by my side, in a different circumstance, but both of us were able to come through and say, "Once again, we made it."

What is your purpose in all of this, God? I wondered again for the hundredth time. I was clinically dead and could have been in heaven forever with you, and you brought me back. What is the message that you are giving me about what I saw? Still no answers, but peace flooded over me.

Yet there were questions running through my mind. Someone would have to get me through this. Surely Pastor Ed would understand what happened, I thought, but I have to tell Ronnie about the rest of what I have seen first. He will let me know how safe it is to share.

As I lay there processing all that had happened in the past few days, a perfect picture suddenly came to my mind. A wounded soldier on a cot was being lifted by his comrades and carried away in the midst of enemies everywhere. My eyes filled with tears as I saw this picture in my mind's eye. I sensed the danger all around and knew this was hostile, dangerous territory that the wounded soldier was being carried through. And just like that, the picture was gone. I knew God had just assured me that He had brought me through hostile ground.

"For the Lord your God goes with you; He will never leave you nor forsake you" (Deuteronomy 31:6b). That Scripture kept pressing against my mind. God wanted me to know, as bad as the place was that I had seen, He was with me through it all. He never left my side.

I prayed, Lord, I feel like a soldier. What I saw has left me shell-shocked. What am I to do with this? Why did you want me to see this place? And then a doubt sneaked into my mind: God, I am saved, aren't I? Are you trying to tell me something?

He assured me in my thoughts, just as He had when I stood in that place. "You are an onlooker to this scene. You have been saved by the blood of the Lamb."

***

Calmed and comforted by the promise in those words, my mind turned to memories of a young mother and farmer's wife, who years ago came back to the God who never left her as she wandered away from a close relationship with him.

He Was There All the Time

Until my heart had stopped beating a few days before, I hadn't had any experiences with seeing anything in the spiritual world. I had felt spiritual happenings, though—for example, the time shortly after I rededicated my life to the Lord, when I was around twenty-four.

I had been to a Women's Aglow meeting after my pastor's wife had invited me. I had walked away from God for eight years, and He had been so patient with me, gently wooing me back to Him. It was in the middle of winter. I had two little boys by that time, and I was a desperate mama. We had started dairy farming a few years prior so Ronnie was out a lot. It was primarily my responsibility to raise these two boys, I thought, since his work was very demanding.

During that winter we had a lot of sickness in our family. It seemed as though we caught every virus that came along. Unfortunately, about that time my wisdom teeth were also giving me a lot of problems. My dentist decided it was time to remove them. Bad timing, I realized afterwards—my immune system was shot. I was sick and fatigued constantly. It was physically draining just keeping up with two active little boys.

My parents were spending most of their winters in Texas helping at a mission. I missed my mother terribly. I felt bad calling Ronnie's mother because I knew she was busy. I tried to be independent and run on what little strength I still possessed.

One day I remember just walking through the toy-scattered house, seeing dirty dishes stacked precariously on the kitchen counter. I had not showered for two days and I looked like a zombie. I got to our hallway and collapsed. I don't know how long I lay there. When I awakened,

I remember the two boys jumping over me as though we were playing a new game. I couldn't laugh at how much fun they were having. I just knew I was sick and on the verge of losing my mind.

It wasn't long after that when a friend invited me back to church. I needed something, and I knew it would be a start in the right direction.

It was the same church where I was raised. There was a Spirit-filled pastor leading the congregation with a wife who I immediately felt was kin to the angels. God's love was so evident in their lives.

Ronnie often could not go to church with us because he was still putting long hours into the farm. I would gather the boys, and we showed up every time the church doors opened. My favorite time was a Wednesday night when our pastor led a Bible study and a time of praise and worship. I felt as though I had stepped back into the little white church where I had first met the Lord. I realized God had never left me; I was the one who had walked away. He was meeting me with open arms.

It wasn't long after I began going back to church that our pastor's wife invited some of us women to the Women's Aglow meeting where I responded to God's call to come back to Him. I was so hungry for female companionship that I gladly accepted. When I walked into the meeting, I was blown away. The Holy Spirit was there in a big way. I could do nothing but cry. I didn't know until then how much I had missed God. I rededicated my life to Him that day.

That night, I was awakened from a sound sleep. I don't know how to describe the feeling, but something "spiritual" was happening around my bed. I sensed something in my room, and it wasn't good. I wanted to wake up Ronnie, but I was paralyzed with fear. I couldn't move. The words of my friend, Donna, once again came to my mind: "Call out the name of Jesus!"

I tried to utter His name. It was as though my voice was somehow trapped inside. I whispered, "Jesus!" again, "Jesus!" My voice barely came out. I kept on saying His name until my voice was audible.

Whatever kept Ronnie from hearing me to this day I don't understand. I don't know how many times I prayed Jesus' name that night, but after a while, the evil spiritual presence was gone. When I shared the experience with my pastor later, he told me that spiritual darkness hates losing a person's soul to God. The Enemy was trying whatever he could that night to attack. He didn't want me going back to God. God was there that night, though. Just as He promises, "He will never leave us."

I had known the spiritual world was real, but I hadn't experienced it before. That night my ears were opened. I heard movement and sensed a presence. I just didn't see anything.

As the night slowly pressed on towards dawn in the quiet purposefulness of the hospital wing, I remembered how I had called on Jesus and He had come to my aid that night so many years ago. It was certain that what had happened to me a couple days ago as I lay on the ground being brought back to life was different. God had opened my eyes to see something few on this earth ever witness. I knew this vision was huge. I couldn't keep silent, but I would protect it until the time was right.

***

I don't know how much sleep I got that night as all of these thoughts ran through my mind. I couldn't believe it when I glanced out the window and saw the first hint of daylight.

Our Easter Miracle

It was Saturday morning, the day before Easter. What would this day bring, I wondered. In a little while, the cardiologists began making their 6:00 a.m. rounds. Often they encouraged me to get up and move around to prevent blood clots from forming in the legs. They lamented with me about not having the defibrillator implanted on Friday and told me what I already knew—that I'd have to stay through the weekend to wait for surgery on Monday. I know they felt badly about it, but emergencies come first. They checked my heart, read my chart, and patiently answered my questions. This process was getting to be routine by now.

"Nothing new, we'll see you tomorrow unless there are any changes," and out my door they went to see the next patient.

I clicked on the TV and mindlessly scrolled through the channels to find something to pass the time. After a while, the breakfast cart came around. I welcomed the food and ate heartily. When that was done, I knew I had to move around some. I was always careful to take my time getting up. The medicine the doctors put me on would change my blood pressure; as a result, they had cautioned me to take my time rising from a sitting position. After I got up, I made the familiar walk around the hallway. I walked back to a window where there was a good view of a helicopter landing. As I watched it, I thought about the day I had arrived. Was there maybe another patient watching through the copter window? I said a prayer for whoever it was. Perhaps someone had said a prayer watching me that day.

Around midmorning, my cousin Martha and her family from the eastern shore of Virginia came in for a visit. She had visited my mom in Richmond, Virginia, when she was a patient at Medical College of Virginia, shortly before she died. I believe, in every family, that some loyal family members always come through—people like Martha and her children. She and her daughter, son-in-law and granddaughter came in my room carrying gifts and smiles.

"Go ahead, Teresa, open them. We thought you could use these." As I took the wrapping paper off one of the presents, I was taken aback. It was a beautiful floral gown and a bright pink robe with matching slippers. This same cousin had blessed my mother with a beautiful gown during her stay at MCV. My mother and I had been alike in many ways. One of the ways is that we owned very few nice gowns. We wore the same tattered ones over and over. A stay in the hospital caught us both by surprise. God must have put it on our cousin's heart to make such a purchase.

Tears filled my eyes as I hugged Martha, while I thought about about how my mother must have felt opening her gift twenty years earlier while lying in her hospital bed with the same heart condition. It was one of those emotional moments.

Martha and her family stayed for around an hour. I relived the events of the past Monday as I explained what had happened. Martha had been close to my mother, and I knew she would appreciate the fact that I had seen my mother and Mark. The silence that followed after I finished lingered as each one captured the images I had just described.

As I was becoming more comfortable in sharing my story, I began to notice something more and more: I began getting the distinct impression that it gave people hope. I knew Martha was a believer, and I sensed how comforting my experience must have been to her. As we each sat with tear-rimmed eyes, we consoled one another with stories about my mother and brother. Martha's daughter, Kelly, had been about the same age as Mark. The two of them had played together as children at family picnics. It was good to laugh over some of the funny stories and somehow comforting to cry as we realized those days had been good ones.

Martha's family's time grew to a close. I was sorry to see them go, but they promised to stay in touch. We waved our goodbyes, and I leaned back on my pillow and dozed a little afterward.

I spent the rest of the day visiting with more family and friends. Since this was a Saturday, people had the weekend off. My brother Reggie, his wife Sue, and their three delightful, bubbly girls came back to Virginia from Charlotte for Easter weekend. After a while, more of my family came in. It grew to a point that there wasn't enough room for everyone, and we moved to the end of the hall in a waiting room. I felt very awkward dragging the IV stand around with me and wearing the big heart monitor around my neck, but I knew these were necessary devices. I carried a cup of ice water with me to relieve my cough.

As we sat together visiting, the afternoon went by quickly. More people flocked in, as word had gotten around our community that I had been clinically dead and then resuscitated. People were prompted to come see me. This just didn't happen very often.

Then Carlton's pastor, Dave, stopped by. He had been with our family on Monday and was one of the prayer warriors who had interceded for me. It was so good to see him. There was a certain aura around that man. After some of the people began leaving, Pastor Dave asked if I'd like any Scripture read. I jumped at the chance. "Scripture is my strength right now," I replied. He opened his Bible and read a Scripture that by now was becoming very familiar to me, Psalms 91:9-16:

> If you make the Most High your dwelling—even the Lord, who is my refuge—then no harm will befall you, no disaster will come near your tent. For he will command his angels concerning you to guard you in all your ways; he will lift you up in their hands, so that you will not strike your foot against a stone. You will tread upon the lion and the cobra; you will trample the great lion and the serpent. "Because he loves me," says the Lord, "I will rescue him; I will protect him, for he acknowledges my name. He will call upon me, and I will answer him; I will be with him in trouble, I will deliver him and honor him. With long life will I satisfy him and show him my salvation.

Pastor Dave closed his Bible and looked up. Of course I had tears streaming down my face. God had done just what He'd promised. He *had* sent His angels to guard me, God had rescued me, He was with me in trouble, and He was promising me a long life. His word is rich in promises. Somehow having it read just seemed to drive the point home even more, especially when I realized God had put that particular Scripture in Pastor Dave's heart. I had read it before and found it comforting, but this time having it read made it stand out like flashing neon lights. God's promises are real.

Visiting with my brother's pastor had been a blessing. As Carlton, Kathy, and Dave started to leave, Kathy handed me a huge basket of Easter candy. She had diligently picked out special treats she knew I liked—or at least, that I used to like, and would again. As they left, I thought, they each brought food here today—chocolate and treats for the physical, and God's rich Word for the spiritual.

The visitors just kept coming! My dad brought in some friends I hadn't seen for a long time. I am a talker by nature, but my cough got so bad at times, that I had to signal for others to talk. My brother, Reggie, somehow sensed that and took over the conversation.

Suddenly one of the RNs rushed into the waiting room. "Mrs. Simmons' monitor is reporting lots of PVCs. Maybe she'd be better back in her room so she can lie down and get some rest." Apparently my constant cough had somehow stimulated my heart. I felt bad for my company, but I knew by this time how frail my heart was and that I needed help. I shuffled back to my room with the assistance of the nurse.

As my friends left, they stopped in my doorway and said a quick goodbye.

"We'll be back tomorrow on our way back to Charlotte," Reggie said, as he, Sue, and the girls left. Dad lingered for a little. He knew he'd have to catch a ride back home with Reggie so he said goodbye and then hugged and kissed me. My dear father. . .he had been so faithful to come see me every day, and I knew the trip was hard on him.

After an hour or so, my cough began subsiding. By the time Ronnie came, I could talk somewhat reasonably. Eric and Rachel came, too, though the farm chores once again didn't permit very long visits. Behind them came Jared, Whitney, Rebecca, and Nate. I tried to be careful not to talk too much, but I told them about who had already been in to see me. It was frustrating at times to want to be part of the conversation and into the visit, yet to know I was so limited. After I'd say a sentence or two, I'd cough and could feel my heart fluttering. I had often heard my dad say as he aged that he had learned he had to pace himself. I guess I was taking a crash course in what this meant.

Flutter. . .flutter. . . flutter. My family talked a while, and then I would. Before, I had ignored the palpitations, not realizing how serious they were. Now, I was mindful of every one. I was concerned any time my heart felt a little different. I continually grappled with fear that Saturday afternoon. It was yet another area I was just going to have to turn completely over to God. My lack of energy and strength were areas, as well, that would have to go into God's hands.

Common sense told me I just had to learn not to over exert. The new "normal" was going to be so different. I was always used to not having anything holding me back. My lack of energy and strength were to be facts of life, not to mention the fluttering of my heart.

Where is all this going to lead me, Lord? I prayed. I thought I was a healthy forty-eight year old, aging gracefully, and now I was stuck in a hospital floor with almost every other patient on the wing around the ages of seventy to eighty—I had seen many of them when I took my walk with Aunt Betty. How could this happen to me at forty-eight?

I couldn't let depression get a grip. I couldn't let fear reign. I reflected on the Scripture Pastor Dave had just read: "With long life will I satisfy him." God had given me this promise. Just a few hours earlier, these words had penetrated into my deepest being. I realized that like so many times before, Satan had tried to come along with fret and worry. He had taken advantage of a wildly beating heart, pushing fear and worry to move right in. "God, keep your scripture ever fresh in my mind," I prayed.

My family helped to take my mind off this anxiety. It was good to hear that life on the farm was going on as usual and that they were being fed well by neighbors and friends. Ronnie opened a lunch cooler he had brought with him. In it were several sandwiches of grilled beef and pork a neighbor had packed for us along with homemade cookies.

"I know you're probably tired of hospital food by now, so Joyce and Elmer sent these," he said as he showed me the contents inside. The sandwiches smelled delicious. Joyce must have known how much I loved homemade cookies, too.

The kids all said that they wouldn't stick around too long. I think it was always comforting for them to see progression in my health, but by the same token, they had busy lives and

Saturday nights are more fun anywhere else besides a hospital. They told their dad they would leave a vehicle for him and said their goodbyes.

"Sorry, kids, I guess the Easter bunny won't be stopping by the farm tonight," I said. Jared's girlfriend looked at me with a twinkle in her eye and said, "Oh, I don't know about that."

What was she up to, I wondered. Later the next day, she sent a huge basket with my favorite chocolate, an Easter egg dyeing kit, a pastel-colored coffee mug, and other goodies tucked in. She and Rachel had gone shopping together and got Eric's, Jared's, Rebecca's, and Ronnie's favorite candies. They had found their Easter baskets tucked away in a closet off the bedroom, and had filled them as well. What sweet girls! Things carry on. God was putting it on people's hearts to continue specific duties. I didn't need to be anxious over anything.

I was able to sit back on my bed that evening with my husband as we each nibbled on the delicious sandwiches our neighbors had sent. What a nice treat, I thought. I guess it had been the first meal my husband and I had eaten together after almost a week. I knew he couldn't stay long, though. The dairy farm chores would soon be calling.

I savored the moments as long as I could. We each ate one of the scrumptious cookies, and in spite of my lack of interest in sweets, they tasted good. Ronnie wanted to leave the rest of the sandwiches with me, but I convinced him to take them. As good as they were, my appetite still wasn't back and I had all I could eat. He left the cookies for later.

"My mom and dad have an Easter lunch planned for after church tomorrow," he said. "I'll have Mom fix up a plate for you," he said.

"It's OK, Ronnie, you all need time to celebrate Easter. I'll get to celebrate it soon." I kissed him goodbye and once again bade him to be careful crossing the mountain. I spent the rest of the night flipping through TV channels and reading. Restlessness was definitely setting in, but I knew the time wouldn't be much longer. Somehow, the night passed, but it was another sleepless one.

At 6:00 the next morning, Dr. Bergin, my cardiologist, came into my room, and after seeing I was going to begin asking my unending questions, he leaned back against my windowsill. As I reflected back on Monday with him, I touched lightly on the fact that I had seen my mother and brother.

Dr. Bergin was usually quick with an answer, but this time he seemed pensive for a moment. "Your story is definitely a miracle story, and what more appropriate time of the year than this?" He said.

What a wonderful comment to make on Easter morning! On the day on which we celebrate the miracle Jesus' resurrection, he reminded me that I had experienced my own miracle of coming back from the dead. How appropriate that my trip from death back to life should happen at the beginning of the week Christians celebrate the risen Son!

It blessed me to hear a doctor say such a thing. A man God has given a gift to understand some of the complexities of the human body admitted that there are miracles still. After checking my chart and listening to my heart, he began walking out, and he turned and said, "I'm off to church after while." I was amazed to hear many nurses say the same thing that day. It was good to hear them. It made one yearn for church on this Easter morning even more—but it was a worshipful experience just to reflect on what Jesus' resurrection means to the world.

After breakfast, I slipped on the new pink robe on that Martha had brought. I smiled to myself, thinking if I couldn't wear a pretty Easter dress today, at least I'd wear a pretty robe. As I walked out of my room, I was impressed with all the spring-like pastel colors the nurses were wearing. They were bustling about in and out of rooms as I made my walk around the hallways. Even if I was in a hospital, I was going to enjoy this Easter Sunday. The colors lifted my heart, and I took a walk to the window overlooking the helicopter pad. No one there. I walked into the waiting room to look out the other side of the building. I intentionally made myself walk around for the exercise. By now I was hearing that gradually getting into an exercise routine would help improve the function of my heart. I still felt frail, but better each day.

I returned to my room after a while. I stood and enjoyed all the pretty flowers that friends and family had brought and sent. I looked at the big Easter baskets of candy and goodies. Love was reflected in these gifts, sent by people who said they loved and cared for me. I stood there thinking about God's love. I couldn't hold back the tears.

"God, all of these people have sent and brought in tokens of their love, and yet Yours is the best, the gift of Your Son, of new life." The fact that He had spared my life that very week came back in an overwhelming flood of emotions. God had spared me. God had let me come back. I was at death's door, and God showed me something powerful. My work was not finished. Those words hung on in my mind, and I knew it would not be long before I would have the opportunity to share my Easter miracle with people outside my circle of family and close friends.

But for the moment, sleep sounded good. I climbed back into the hospital bed and drifted off for a morning nap.

Easter is Still Easter, Even in the Hospital

A soft metallic jingle and a knock on the partially closed door awakened me. "Mrs. Simmons, would you like your lunch?" The young server lowered my bedside tray to a height from which I could eat sitting up. The hospital food would just have to take the place of a home-cooked meal, I thought. Just as I uncovered the lid, my in-laws Bill and Phyllis walked in with Ronnie. They were carrying a plate of food from their Easter meal. What a welcome sight!

They had eaten early so that they could get to the hospital by lunch time. As I ate, they talked and visited. After I finished, I suggested that we go to the waiting room. My room just felt so small when company came.

And then I had another coughing spell. I tried to let them do most of the talking. My father-in-law has always had a stash of hard candy, but I didn't realize until that day that he even carries a stash with him. After hearing my cough, he emptied his coat and pants pockets of all the hard candy he had. It seemed to soothe my throat.

Letting me rest my throat, they carried on the conversation. They talked about what they had planted in their garden. Both of my in-laws are avid gardeners. They assured me that they would help get mine started. I knew even as the independent person I am, that I had to accept help. The conversation covered various subjects, mainly about the way everyone was pulling together and helping on the farm. They were hard-core farmers who especially knew the importance of help from others. After a while, I glanced at Ronnie and his eyes were closed. He was catching a much deserved nap so I left him dozing in the chair. He slept until my brother Reggie, Sue, and their girls came into the room. They were heading back to Charlotte and just as they had promised, stopped in to say their goodbyes. It wasn't long until my other two brothers and families and my dad arrived. It was a full room and lots of conversation was going on. I tried to behave myself and not talk too much, but it was hard to do, as I enjoyed the company.

Everyone stayed for a few hours and then began filtering out. It wasn't long before Ronnie said they would be leaving. "Have you heard anything about your surgery tomorrow?" he asked. When a nurse came in to check my blood pressure we inquired about it and she said it was hard to determine a time yet, but her guess was that it would be early since they had put me off on Friday. Everyone, including me, was anxious to have it done. Dad and the others promised their prayers as they said their goodbyes. Ronnie assured me that he would be over early the next day in case they did decide to take me in the morning. He and his parents walked me back to my room and bid me farewell.

I sank back again into my bed. "A Sunday afternoon nap would be nice," I thought. Just as I dozed off, I heard someone at my doorway. I looked up and there stood my 6'4" son, Jared. He told me Whitney had gone back to her home and he thought I could use some company. He sat down and talked about some of the training horses he was working with. His work with horses usually kept him busy and didn't allow much time for help on the dairy. I knew, though, this particular week he was stretching himself. Everyone was. As he sat and we talked, I valued this time. Jared is generally my quiet one, and this was one of those rare moments when it was just he and I in uninterrupted conversation. It was a treasure. At times when my cough wouldn't allow talking, Jared would sit quietly. He just seemed to enjoy hanging out with his mom. When he rose to say goodbye, I glanced at the clock; he had been there for three hours! As he leaned down to kiss me goodbye, his cheek was wet with a tear. My grown son, my rugged horse training boy, tough on the outside but tender inside. His eyes were still glistening when he walked out my door.

I barely had time to regroup myself when Rebecca and Nate walked in. She told me all about their day and what they had done. Life is always exciting for her, and she reflected it in her conversation. There's never a dull moment with my bubbly, sanguine daughter. She and Nate were proud at how well they were keeping things at the house orchestrated. She assured me that they were writing down the food people were bringing and tidying up every day for company. My little girl, who used to play house with her friends, now had a real life experience. When I did finally get home, I was very proud at how well she and Nate had done.

She talked about how hard Eric and Rachel were working on the farm. She was impressed with how readily Rachel was willing to do dirty farm work, work that Rebecca abhorred. "You know that's why I'm in the house doing work there, don't you?"

I had to laugh. I guess everyone was adjusting and doing what had to be done. She said Eric and Rachel probably wouldn't be over because they were still doing farm chores. I'm sure Eric was doing extra so that his dad could come to the hospital. We visited for a little while, and then they felt I was getting tired and decided to leave. They mentioned that they'd probably not make a trip the next day as I may not feel up to the company. We hugged and said goodbye.

The day had turned out beautifully, I thought, as they left. I felt thankful that my children were so willing to set aside their responsibilities and their busy lives to come and sit with me. I never wanted to make my children feel any kind of pressure to do that—I wanted them to decide when or if they should come. I had earlier shared that thought with Rebecca, and I think it relieved her.

The evening came and went uneventfully with no more company, no more phone calls, but just a quiet, relaxing Easter evening. I knew as I ate my dinner that I would not be getting any more food until after surgery the next day. One of the nurses told me not to eat or drink anything after midnight.

Then I remembered my neighbor's cookies. Maybe I could have a midnight snack, I thought. Even though my sweet tooth hadn't returned, that cookie tasted really good that night. I was able to fall asleep after that.

Lord, Get Me through This

Sleep didn't last long, though. I glanced at the clock and I tried to guess how many hours until my surgery. I clicked on the TV: "Nutrivita-Whatcha-McCall It Cream has made me look twenty years younger," announced one impossibly thin pop singer, while on another channel a former Mr. Universe demonstrated how to use an expensive exercise machine. Not much else. It was so frustrating not being able to sleep. I knew I couldn't get up and walk around or eat or drink anything. Somehow the time managed to slip by, and in between some of the short naps, I saw the sun rising.

Before long, the cardiologists would be making their rounds. I thought maybe once I saw activity, time would go by more quickly. At precisely 6:00 a.m. one of the cardiologists appeared. He checked my heart and explained the procedure they would be doing. Just as the nurses had said the night before, he didn't know an exact time to expect surgery.

Tick, tick, tick. The clock kept time to my thoughts as I tried to pass the time. No breakfast once again, so I would have to rule out eating. I picked up my Bible. "Please, God give me your words of comfort," I breathed. There they were: "Cast your cares on the Lord and He will sustain you, He will never let the righteous fall," and Psalms 56:3: "When I am afraid, I will trust in you." God's Word helped me uplift my spirits and my faith, and the time passed more easily.

I glanced up when I heard someone at my door; it was Ronnie. He had turned all of the farm duties over to Eric and Rachel. "I didn't know if they'd taken you yet," he said, seeming somewhat relieved. I was glad he had come. It helped having him with me as the morning passed with no one coming in to say they were ready to operate.

Lunchtime came. "We still haven't heard anything, Mrs. Simmons," the nurse would announce as he or she checked on my vitals every hour.

Tick, tick, tick. They asked Ronnie if he wanted something to eat. He turned down the offer, saying he felt bad eating in front of me. I assured him I'd be all right, but he insisted that he'd wait.

Shortly, after 1:00 p.m. a nurse came into my room and announced they were ready for me. Following her was the electrophysiology (EP) doctor who would be doing the procedure. They told my husband I'd probably be gone about one hour.

My heart rate began increasing. I knew I had to remember God's Word and not be afraid. Ronnie and I grabbed hands, and he assured me that I was going to be all right. Having him say that reduced my anxiety.

As I was rolled into the room where the surgery would take place, the attendant talked about the procedure in more detail. She was very thorough, explaining each step beforehand. As she told what medicines would be used, in walked the attending physician. He shook my hand and cracked some jokes about the medicines. His humor lightened my mood. Before long, the EP doctor who performed the surgery told me he would numb the area to be opened where the defibrillator would be placed and that I would be awake during the procedure because they needed to test the device. I would then be given some amnesia medicine so that I wouldn't remember the ordeal as my heart would be shocked back into rhythm.

Now hold on a minute—that thought was a little disturbing to me. To think I'd have to go back into cardiac arrest was not a pleasant one. However, I didn't have a lot of time to dwell on my thoughts, as I could feel the doctor inserting a needle into my left chest. Then he began making an incision.

Not long after he started, he commented on the toughness of my skin. It felt as though he'd cut and then tug. He kept saying I had the toughest skin of anyone he'd ever operated on.

"Dura mater," he said. "Do you know what that means? It's Latin for 'tough mother;" you are one tough mother! He exclaimed, making us laugh even in the middle of the seriousness of what he was doing. It was good that I could laugh along with the staff as they cracked jokes, lightening an otherwise nerve-wracking ordeal. The medicine was very effective; I didn't feel any pain, just pressure.

The EP doctor continued explaining, along with the attendant, each step that followed.

Soon it was time to test the device. I gripped the table, momentarily thinking about my heart going back into arrest. The anesthesiologist told me it wouldn't seem but a second.

"Here we go," he said. I was knocked out with the amnesia medicine. Sure enough it seemed just a second later that he was leaning over saying, "OK. It works. You did fine." Just like that. The finishing procedure also didn't take long. The involved, complicated part was over. All of the staff commented how quickly the surgery took, less than an hour.

I was rolled back into my room by 2:00 p.m. to meet my husband again. He smiled a big smile of relief. Then all of the instructions began, including no lifting my left arm, only slight elevation of my body, and no getting out of bed for twelve hours. That would be the killer, I thought. With all the water I had been drinking, the thoughts of a bed pan were depressing. I was finding the need for frequent urination. A bedpan?! How humbling! Somehow, I will survive, I thought. I've made it this far.

One of the nurses brought lunch to me. Ronnie said he had gotten a bite while I was in surgery. By now, I was hungry and ate very heartily. A cup of beloved tea sat before me.

"Oh, I want to drink a quart of tea," I thought. I'll just have to slow down for the next twelve hours, though.

After lunch we watched Westerns on TV. It felt a little as though we were back home, and that thought pacified me. With the low drone of the black and white movie playing in the background, we were both soon lulled to sleep. The next hour was spent in blissful rest. It felt good to do this; I'm sure a lot of it was medicine-induced but it was welcome.

Before long, a nurse was in to check on my incision. Because they had placed an ice pack on it earlier, the area was still numb. My cardiologist came around to check on it, as well. When he noticed that my hospital gown had gotten soaked from the ice pack, he asked a nurse if I could have my gown changed. It was awkward not being able to use my left arm much, but the doctors wanted it kept as still as possible until the leads going down into my heart had a chance to heal. Somehow I managed.

After a few hours, my family began arriving. They were all respectful of the fact that I'd just had surgery and were careful not to visit too long, even though they'd driven an hour just to see me for five minutes. More than one of them expressed relief that the procedure was over. "You and me both," I answered, feeling pretty cheerful considering that my chest had just been sliced into.

As the afternoon passed into evening, Ronnie felt that he should head home. "One more night and you will be back home," he encouraged. "As soon as you know the time you can be released, let me know," he said as he bent down to say his goodbye.

He walked out one more time. I thought, "Hopefully the next time he walks out that door, I'll be with him." The thought was a pleasant one. This time tomorrow I'll be home, I thought. Now if I can just get through the night and handle the stupid bedpan.

As I reflect on the whole eight-day stay, the worst time for me was, without a doubt, that twelve hours after surgery. I felt the need to urinate every hour, but it was such a bother to get the nurses. It was one of the most humbling ordeals in my life. I watched every minute tick by, and it seemed as though time was standing still.

As the medicine wore off, the pain from the fresh incision became very obvious. I felt miserable. I fidgeted all night. At one point, I buzzed one of the nurses and asked her if there was any way possible I could get up sooner. She wouldn't let me talk her into it. Watching the clock. . .watching the clock. . .I buzzed the nurse the minute the time clicked over to 2:00 a.m. Finally, I thought. I can move! The nurse came into my room and explained that she would have to take my blood pressure while I was lying, sitting, and then standing to make sure that there were no drastic changes. Luckily, I passed that test. As I stood, I felt a little wobbly, but with her assistance, I went straight to the restroom. I felt like screaming, "No more stupid bedpan!" Since the pain was becoming more intense, I asked for some pain medicine. Maybe that would help me get a little rest, I thought. It took the edge off, but barely.

Hallelujah! Seeing the sun rising was such a relief. This is the day I've been waiting for! I thought. With the cardiologists' 6:00 a.m. rounds came instructions for my departure. Before they would let me go, I needed x-rays to make sure that the device and leads were where they needed to be, they explained. "Everything else looks good," they said as my incision was checked. Breakfast time came. My last breakfast here, I thought. Just as I was finishing, two technicians came in to take me for x-rays. It was encouraging to see things moving along. I got into their wheelchair. Please God, let everything be in its proper place, I prayed. I was then taken back to my room.

It wasn't long after that a nurse came and announced that the x-rays looked fine and that the doctors had discharged me. Praise God! I quickly called Ronnie and asked him to come get me. Unfortunately, he was doing the milking chores that morning and he'd have to wait until they were done, he told me. He knew how anxious I was to get home. He assured me that he'd get done as quickly as possible, but then he had to shower and take the one hour trip to get to me.

Again, every minute ticked by slowly, slowly, slowly. I had told the rest of my family not to bother to come as I felt reasonably sure I'd be home that day. I decided after I dressed and packed, I'd walk around some. My strength had been returning more by then.

Just as I finished the last of my packing, my cousin Faye walked in. She had driven quite a ways to get to the hospital. "I'm surprised to see you getting ready to go home today," she said, sounding very pleased about it. "I'll stay and walk around with you awhile," she offered.

By this time, I had been told that I wouldn't be restricted to the cardio department, but could go anywhere I wanted to within the hospital. I knew that even though this was refreshing news, I had to be careful. This would be the most I had walked in eight days since the incident, but I wanted so badly to get out and see some new sights. My cousin and I took the elevator downstairs to the main lobby.

It felt so different to be out walking among people again! Had it been only eight days? It seemed so much longer. I looked around, seeing people young and old, healthy and unhealthy, thin, fat, tired, smiling, worried-looking, as they hurried to whatever was occupying their time in the hospital that day and thought, do these people know what God just did in my life? I wanted to go up to everyone and tell my miracle story.

As my cousin and I walked around, I began noticing how frail my body had become. The trauma my heart had been through was becoming obvious. Whereas before, a walk like our little stroll wouldn't have seemed like anything, suddenly with each step I became weaker. It was scaring me, but I didn't want my cousin to know how weak I was feeling. I was afraid I'd be kept even longer in the hospital. I suggested that we stop to sit and talk. We did, and after fifteen or twenty minutes, I began feeling better. How depressing, I thought. I've barely walked any at all and I feel like a ninety-year-old woman.

By that time the medicine from the surgery the day before was affecting my stomach, and I fought back nausea. I kept all of this to myself, though, praying silently that Ronnie would hurry. I mentioned to my cousin that I was ready to go back to my room. I was really hoping we'd find Ronnie once we returned, but we didn't. I knew he was doing everything in his power to get there as soon as he could, but it was another hour before he arrived. What a welcome sight when he did.

Finally! Homeward bound! We said goodbye to my cousin. Ronnie gathered my belongings, and we thanked all of the nurses. We got on the elevator and continued our journey home. Even though I was still feeling nauseated and very weak, the feeling of anticipation of going home welled up inside. I couldn't wait.

Once we got into the car and began driving away from my home for the past eight days, everything seemed surreal. Did all this really just happen to me? I began wondering. It was a thought that would continue for months ahead.

As we drove through the town of Charlottesville, I realized how much I appreciated the colors of spring in a whole new way. It was as though I was looking at nature for the first time. All of the beautiful spring flowers and foliage in the trees seemed brighter than ever. I kept "wowing" at everything to the point that it made my husband shake his head, smiling at my excitement. "I've been looking at stainless steel and white walls for the past eight days," I said.

In my heart, though, I knew my renewed appreciation for the beauty around me was just a part of something much deeper: The realization of the fact that I had seen what lies beyond death and had been brought back for the time being. I am alive, and life will be totally different for me now, I promised God and myself. And it has—even to this day, the smallest wonder in God's creation makes me stop and breathe a prayer of gratitude to a loving, awesome Creator and to the One who makes such beauty possible for me to enjoy.

As we crossed the Blue Ridge Mountains, Ronnie said the children had been working hard to keep things neat and tidy in and around the house and farm. The children, as well as their friends, had done laundry, cleaned, cooked, ironed, and had helped with farm chores. He knew how much this would mean to me. They had all been telling me this as they came to visit, but Ronnie wanted to reiterate that they had even stayed home from their jobs. Jared had even turned training horses away so that he could help with the various chores.

The one-hour trip home passed quickly as Ronnie told me who had visited. He talked about various activities on the farm, and as always about his future plans for his horses. Again, it just felt like old times. I rode and enjoyed his company as my "farm boy" shared his heart. As we passed the neighboring farms, I was astonished how quickly some of the spring crops were already popping through the ground. All of this had happened in just one week. Life goes on, I thought.

As we turned into the graveled road that leads us to our house, the familiarity of it all sank in. The neighbors' homes were already boasting with their spring accents of flowers and blossoming trees. It was an awesome sight!

When Ronnie turned into our driveway, tears began running down my cheeks. Our faithful farm dogs Yona and Amaya soon greeted our car and ran along beside us. My eyes welled up. "Ronnie, do you know how good it is to be home?"

It just seemed as though it had been so long. Getting out of our car and walking into my house was like the first time. I looked at everything—every sight—every smell—every sound. I was just enjoying it all. As we came through the door, I could see the children had been busy. The house seemed to sparkle of cleanliness. Rebecca had lit candles and placed the gifts of flowers throughout the house. It was such a welcome sight. She and Nate stood proudly in the kitchen as I oohed and aahed over everything. They told me that Eric and Jared were doing farm chores.

Ronnie took my hand and led me to the phone. "Here, I saved all the messages on the answering machine for you," he said.

I sat down in a comfortable chair and listened to each message of hopes, prayers, and expressions of sentiment left behind by loving, caring friends and family. He knew again how much it would mean to me to hear the loving thoughts stored all week. Rebecca and Nate excitedly showed me all the gifts of food that people had brought. I knew we would be eating well and wouldn't have to cook for a while.

The next few days consisted mostly of resting and visiting with friends and family. Various members of our church brought even more food in for us. I could get spoiled not having to cook, I thought.

Each day, more of my strength returned. People tried to be careful not to overstay. Even though I knew I was getting stronger each day, increased palpitations in my heart let me know when I was overdoing it. I had to remember what my dad had been telling himself. "Just pace yourself," he had been saying recently, and I heard his words echo through my mind. They were good words of advice for me, too, I knew. And Ronnie had given me some good advice, as well, though he probably didn't know his straightforward comment about what I had seen was a type of advice: "That's why you're back here with us, then." I had a job to do, and the time was upon me.

What Did It All Mean?

On Thursday of that week, Pastor Ed and Eileen came to see us and brought us supper. It was such a pretty spring day that we decided to visit together outside.

Jared soon brought everyone a glass of freshly made ice tea, crackers, cheese, and chocolates. It was a treat to see my twenty-four-year-old son stepping in as host. As we commented on his generous act of hospitality, we munched on cheese and crackers and sipped our ice tea. It would have made any Southerner really proud.

Ronnie and Pastor Ed paired off into their conversation, and Eileen and I turned to one another. In a serious voice Eileen asked, quietly, "Teresa, how are you, really?" I knew from the tone of her voice she was implying something deeper than the physical. I knew that this was the moment.

Eileen would be a safe choice. I could share with her, but was I ready to share everything yet? I still didn't fully understand everything I had seen. However, I knew I had to start somewhere.

"Eileen," I faltered, "I saw more than my mom and Mark, but I'm not really sure I understand it all, so I'm going to tell you just what I saw and heard."

She moved her chair closer. I stated, "I don't remember how I got to heaven or how I left. I was just suddenly standing before my mother and brother with their outstretched hands, experiencing that feeling and seeing the brilliant light all around them, and just as I stretched my arms out to embrace them, I was taken away. It happened so quickly. Just a glimpse, and I was gone.

"But, Eileen," I continued, "it's the next part that I don't understand. I was taken somewhere else. Suddenly, and I do mean suddenly, I was standing in this place in a somewhat elevated position looking out on this huge mass of people walking in front of me—real people. But these people were terribly frightened. Their faces were distorted with fear and shock. I was crouched down with my hands on my knees to peer into their faces better. I could sense their fear. I became very frightened myself. I wasn't only seeing people, but there were these grey spiritual beings in among the people and on the other side."

I suddenly wondered if Eileen believed me. I knew what I had seen was something incredible to tell someone, but I had seen it. I had to continue, but I realized I wasn't ready to tell it all yet.

"These spiritual beings were somewhat translucent. Like a cloud or mist, they were hooded and they had no faces." (To this day, I hesitate to use the words "grim reaper" but that was the appearance they had.) "I believed they were evil. It looked as though they were herding the people along. There were so many people."

I didn't know how much to tell Eileen. This was new, voicing a story of the most incredible happening that has ever occurred to me. How much should I tell? I hadn't even told Ronnie all of it yet! I felt I could only tell her a little more. I didn't know why I wasn't ready to share everything.

"Eileen, I then heard a voice. I heard, 'Your work is not finished.' When I was taken from there, all I could think of were my children and their salvation. I had to come back and make sure that my family is all saved! What do you think?"

By this time I was trembling inside. Just talking about it caused me to see it all again in my mind's eye.

Eileen sat pensively. She began, "Teresa, God knows how much our children mean to us. I think He wanted to have that impact on you to help you sense the need for salvation for others." She continued, "By causing you to sense the desire for salvation in your children, what was closest to your heart, God was prompting you to come back with a heart for the lost."

Her words penetrated my heart. They resonated into my spirit. I knew they were words spoken by her mouth, but they were actually from the heart of God. Even though I had a tremendous urgency to come back and pray for my family's salvation, it went beyond that. No one, no one, no one, should ever be in that place. It was horrible.

I don't know why I didn't continue with the rest during that conversation with Eileen. It did disturb me to think about all of the details, but I knew Eileen would understand. Maybe somehow, I felt it would betray Ronnie if I shared this with someone else first. Maybe that is why I hesitated. I knew as soon as I could I'd tell Ronnie everything. I couldn't hold back anything, no matter how it felt.

As soon as Ed and Eileen left, I would tell him. I wondered if Eileen knew there was more. She has always been one of those spiritual sisters who seem to know something even without anyone sharing. It often prompted me to share my concerns with her. I knew she and Ed were true prayer warriors.

We finished our conversation with prayer. Ed lifted up thankfulness to God for His grace in restoring my health and he prayed God's continued protection over our family. There was always such a sense of peace and assurance when Ed prayed. They hugged us and said goodbye.

Shortly after they left, our family gathered at the oak kitchen table to enjoy the meal our pastor had just left for us. Food for our stomach and food for our souls, I thought as we dined together. The meal was delicious, and the company was divine. It was so good to be back home.

Rebecca and Rachel announced after supper that they would clean up everything. It was nice not having to think about dirty dishes for a while. Each person went his own way. As evening continued, farm chores would soon have to be started. I wondered if Ronnie would have time for me to share my story with him, and I didn't want to feel rushed through it.

I felt up to a walk. Since Ronnie had already left the house, I decided to go in that direction.

"You Betcha I'll Share!"

Someone asked me if I have seen any changes in Teresa since she came home. She is a lot more understanding toward other people—not that she wasn't before, but now she's more caring even than before and little things don't seem to bother her. People seem to look to her for help or for spiritual advice. The biggest thing, though, I've learned from her experience is how small and short-lived problems are here on this earth. So many things that seemed important before are not so now. Life has a completely different perspective.

—Ronnie Simmons

I found Ronnie outside the dairy barn, or "the parlor," as we jokingly called it. "Ronnie, could I talk to you?"

By this time I felt that if I didn't share my story, I was going to burst. I couldn't hold it in any longer. He stopped and crawled up on the four wheeler, and sat there waiting.

"Sure, Teresa."

"Ronnie . . ." Where do I start, I began wondering. "I don't really know how to tell you this, but I shared some of it with Eileen today, and I feel I've got to tell you about it." He looked interested and inquisitive. I continued awkwardly, "I went somewhere else besides heaven, and I don't fully understand it. I don't know why I couldn't share all of the details with Eileen today, but I'm going to share all of it with you."

After being married to Ronnie for twenty-eight years, I knew I should feel comfortable describing every aspect of what had happened and what I had seen. It was just that this was so different. If this had happened in the physical world, people could identify with it, I rationalized. This was spiritual—it was so totally different.

I told him what I had told Eileen. "What I didn't tell her, and I guess I didn't because I don't know how significant it is, is that after seeing Mom and Mark I was taken to this 'place.'

"The first thing, or things, I saw were these two huge spiritual beings standing in front of me with their arms stretched out just as I had seen Mom and Mark do. I suddenly heard in my mind, or more like an understanding, I heard an explanation: 'Mockery—they're mocking your mother and brother.'

"Ronnie, it was as if they had just seen Mom and Mark and then they were stretching out their arms. I somehow knew they were more powerful than the other spiritual beings I saw. They looked very similar, but they were bigger. I don't know how I knew they held a higher position than the smaller ones; somehow I sensed this. They were big, nine or ten feet tall and gray.

"I was confused. I thought, how can this be; I was right before my mother and brother at the entrance of heaven and now I'm here at this place . . . . I felt my spirit ask, 'Lord, where am I? I thought I was saved.' I never had a conversation, but as soon as I would have a thought, there would be an answer in my understanding. Immediately an answer came to my mind, or more like a thought. 'You are saved, you are an onlooker only.'

"It was then that I saw all of those people. Ronnie, if you go back to the legal pad the nurses gave me at the hospital and read it, it was on there. I wrote, 'I saw many people who died.' That's what I meant, but knew I couldn't explain it then. Those people, they were so, so afraid. There were so many of them. They looked so shocked."

I told him about the other grey spiritual beings, just as I had told Eileen. "They scared me so badly. It was like they were moving the people on. Just when I crouched down to really see into the people's faces, two of the people looked right at me. I felt sorrow like I've never felt before. Their eyes were pleading. They wanted me to do something. Ronnie, it was very obvious they knew I wasn't supposed to be there. One of them was an elderly man, tall and bald, the other was a middle-aged woman, brunette and brown-eyed, very beautiful. I remember thinking, she's so pretty.

"I wanted to help them, but fear immobilized me. I don't know how long I stood there looking. Time seemed so different. I just remember a fear as I've never had before. At that time, these spiritual beings turned and looked at me. I sensed they were going to come over toward me.

"Ronnie, all at once I felt all of this energy start to surround me. *Energy* is the only way I can explain it. I knew intuitively it was some type of a transit. It was such a strange sensation. I also knew somehow, that we (I know Christ was by my side) were going through enemy territory. I remember praying things like 'Jesus, don't leave me, Jesus, stay by my side' over and over.

"I don't know how long I was in this place; I don't know how long the transit from the place back to my body took. I just remember getting awake and seeing the two doctors in their white lab coats standing over me, and the one asking, 'If you can hear me, squeeze my finger.'

"I did, mightily. I didn't want to go back to that horrible, horrible place. I wanted to make sure those doctors kept me right where I was. Ronnie, I don't understand all of this. God has never allowed me to see anything like this ever. Why me? What am I supposed to do with this? I don't really know where that place was. I have so many questions about it all." I could have continued on and on.

I could tell Ronnie really didn't know how to answer me, but I could also tell he believed me. He knew me—he knew

I'm not into sensationalism. He sat on the four-wheeler and slowly replied, "I think you should share all of this with Pastor Ed; he may know, but I don't know what to say."

I knew he was right. That meant I'd have to wait a week before our next Bible study because I wouldn't be able to see Ed in person before then. At the doctor's instructions I could not drive anywhere for a few weeks—and my problem was that I wanted an immediate understanding. I did not want to tell Ed all of this over the phone. Not knowing what the experience meant or where I had been was becoming increasingly frustrating.

Then I stopped myself for a moment: Eileen will share with Pastor Ed the things I told her, I realized. Be patient. God's timing will come. Uncannily, Ed called the next day. He asked if I could share my story at church on Sunday. He probably sensed the excitement in my voice as I replied, "I'd love to, Ed. I'll never be able to sit on that back pew the same. I have a story to tell. You betcha I'll share!"

The Milkmaid and Her Husband Speak

We get invited to speak at a lot of groups these days, and when Teresa begins to speak, I still can hardly keep my composure. It's still very real to me.
—Ronnie Simmons

I have to say something: I've never been a public speaker. I have never felt comfortable in groups, especially to get up and say anything. In the past when I was asked to present teachers' awards at school functions, my stomach was raw from nervousness. If I had to speak on behalf of a committee on which I served, I would beg out of getting up and reporting anything.

How had I so boldly and confidently told Ed I would get up in front of the congregation at church and share my testimony? It had to be the boldness of Christ. He had done something huge and marvelous in my life; how could I not share it?

But how much do I tell? I began wondering. "How do I share something I don't fully understand?" I asked Ronnie.

"You just share what you think you ought to," was his answer. Boy, this was going to take some prayer.

As I came into contact with people over the next few days, I begged for prayer. I also prayed, "God, I can't mess this up. You sent me back for a reason, allow me to do it right." I prayed every waking hour until Sunday rolled around. When that morning arrived, I have to admit I was nervous, but I felt confident. God had given me a message, a miracle. He would see that it was told; He just needed a willing vessel. I prayed, "Let me be your mouthpiece; let me say exactly what you want said."

I was still somewhat sore and fatigued from the trauma my body had been through. It had been only fourteen days since I had lay without a pulse on the ground at our farm, and only six since having the defibrillator implanted, but God gave me an amazing strength that day. The cough had continued to linger. I asked different people to pray that I could get through my story without coughing. I carried my bottle of water with me.

As we arrived at church, Ed encouraged us to sit near the front, something we never do. We're always late getting to church because of the farm chores, and we would usually slide into the back pew. This would be different. All of my family and all of Ronnie's family came with us that Sunday. Generally Dad, my siblings, and Ronnie's family have their own churches where they worship. Their support over the last two weeks had meant so much to me and it didn't stop with my coming home.

After an awesome praise and worship time, Ed gave announcements. He covered the usual formalities. I sat amazed at the sweet peace that God was allowing me to experience. Generally by that point I would be a nervous bundle, but a very unusual calmness kept me still and encouraged. Ed gave a short introduction. In a little while, he asked Ronnie and me to both come forward. Ed laid his hands on us and asked God's blessing on our words. This was one of those times that there was no mistaking the presence of the Holy Spirit. He was everywhere in that church atmosphere that day. Thinking back on it still gives me chills.

As I started to share, it was just as though God was giving me the words to say. Even a milkmaid like me can be of value to God's kingdom, I thought. I had no notes; I shared just as God allowed me. For whatever reasons, I did not talk about seeing all of those people or the gray spiritual beings. Instead, I shared that I had seen my mother and Mark, that I had sensed the glorious presence and feeling, and then that I had heard God's declaration, "Your work is not finished."

I talked about the physical happenings; how significantly low my chances were at surviving; the fact that I was coded and had a .02 percent chance and then of going into pulseless electrical activity and having less than a five percent chance; experiencing cardiogenic shock and beating the odds of only twenty percent surviving, and then having my lungs filled with blood and fluid and my brain deprived of oxygen. Last, I talked about coming back with little effect on my body. I was not supposed to be alive! God wanted me back because I had a story to tell!

Then it was Ronnie's turn, and he shared his side. He explained how he felt, how he immediately jumped into doing CPR—he said he just "did what I've seen people do on TV and what I remembered from seeing it done once in high school"—and how all the timing lined right up. He added more humor in telling that he found the dog licking my face. He could share things I couldn't. He had been there firsthand and had seen things in the physical world. I had seen the spiritual world.

I shared what I felt led to share before those people we all knew and loved. When we both finished speaking, Ed asked our families to come forward. Different members of the church came up as well, as they all prayed over our family. Ed prayed that God would use this story to bring Him glory, and he prayed healing over me and our family.

Thanks to God, I was able to share what had happened and didn't have to cough one time! When we turned to go back to our seats, a glorious clap and a standing ovation cheered on the work of the Lord. God is awesome! He had shown a mighty work and gave a glimpse of a "foretaste of glory divine." There were no dry eyes that day.

Later I asked myself a crucial question about why I only shared the "good" part of what I had seen. Was I holding back the rest, or did God not want me to share that yet? The answer eluded me for the moment, but it would come in time.

Time to Tell the Rest of the Story

I knew I had to tell everything, however hard to believe it was. It simply had to be told. At our next Bible study, Ronnie encouraged me to tell Ed and our group the rest of what I had seen. In this setting, it felt right to share. Everyone wanted to know the whole story.

"I still don't know where I was taken," I began hesitantly. As I continued I began to speak more clearly, and I shared every detail except one: I held back the part about the two bigger spiritual bodies. Why? I'm not sure. For one thing, though, I really didn't know how significant they were and I'd need to talk to someone about them first.

People began offering possible explanations for what I had seen. Then Ed turned his Bible to Revelation 20:11-15 and shared verse 12: "And I saw the dead . . ." He offered that as perhaps an explanation. We discussed it as a group and the other aspects of my journey. Everyone had questions. I wanted so badly to just take everything I had seen and impart that image to everyone. Still to this day, I wish I had some way of transferring the images of what I saw into the minds of people I talk to. I am convinced if everyone could actually see for themselves what I saw, no one would ever want to go there.

Over the next few weeks, the question continued hanging over my mind. "Lord, where was this?" I prayed for an answer. I tried to explain it to myself. I thought about David's words in Psalm 23. I turned to my Bible and read that chapter. I thought about verse 4: "Even though I walk through the valley of the shadow of death, I will fear no evil, for you are with me. . ." I asked God, "Is this where I was?" Was I walking through the valley of the shadow of death? And there must be evil there; David mentioned that.

People were also very curious about the voice I heard telling me my work was not yet done. At one of the places I shared my story a lady came up to me and asked, "What did the voice sound like?"

I had to tell her, "I can't say it sounded like a 'so and so' voice; I just know it was a very familiar voice, a voice my spirit recognized. I don't know how else to explain it. I think of the apostle Paul, who says, ". . .the Spirit himself intercedes for us with groans that words cannot express" (Romans 8:26) and where Jesus promises, "My sheep listen to my voice" (John 10:27) and that if we are His sheep, we follow Him because we know His voice (John 10:4). I knew that voice, though I can't point to a particular person who sounds like what I heard.

Another area of curiosity was about who the frightened man and woman were looking at when they looked towards me. Did they actually see *me*?

At a Bible study, one of the men commented, "Were they looking at you, or did they see Christ?" That was something I hadn't thought about until then. Sometime later in one of the churches where I shared my story, one of the ladies came up to me and presented a similar thought: "When the elderly man and the middle-aged lady turned and looked at you pleadingly, do you think maybe they were looking at Christ?" My heart skipped a beat or two.

Thinking about this question, I remembered something Pastor Ed has often said: We are "Jesus in the skin." Here on this side, I can share my testimony, I can plead with people and I can pray for their souls. I can be Jesus in the skin now. After this life, it is too late. He has given me a burden for the lost that will not go away. So maybe the man and woman did see Jesus—but it was too late for them to become one of His.

As I shared my testimony in churches over the next few weeks, I would give a detailed account of the physical aspects of my experience—the low percentage of those who survive, the very high possibility of brain damage even if someone does survive, and then the spiritual aspect of what I'd seen. I always followed with an invitation to the lost to come to Christ. I am confident that this is why I'm back; God has given me a burden for the lost, the seeking, and the hurting.

On one particular Sunday as I was driving to one of our local churches to share my story, the verse from Psalms 126:5 came to my mind: "Those who sow in tears will reap with songs of joy." It just seemed to come from nowhere and settled in my mind. "OK, Lord, now what does that mean?" No answer came, at least not yet. I got to the church, and the presence of God was felt by everyone. I shared my story as God gave me the words and thoughts. As always, I felt led to give an invitation to anyone who didn't have a relationship with Christ. People began coming forward. As the pastor, the elders, and I prayed with people, a young woman came up to me with tears in her eyes, followed by her husband and his father. They tearfully shared how the husband of the young woman had just come to know the Lord as a result of my story and they thanked me for boldly sharing it.

"They. . .will reap with songs of joy. . ." That family's tears were tears of joy. The father excitedly told how many years they had wept and prayed for the salvation of his son, and today he had made a step to know Christ. The joy in their tears led me to tears, too, as we embraced one another.

"That's what you meant, Lord," I whispered. Events of this nature happened countless times in the next year as I continued to tell my story. God would often give me a nugget of something, in the form of verse, a song, a thought, whatever, and then expound on it later as only God can.

When I was in the hospital, first in ICU and then in the cardiac unit, I guarded what I had seen, both the lovely images and the horrifying ones, as precious jewels. I knew what I had witnessed was something spectacular that God had allowed. I knew the right moment, the right people, the right setting would have to come along soon. I had thought I would burst until I shared it. I knew it was real—that God had allowed me to step over from this physical world, as we know it, into the spiritual.

Sharing those jewels became my reason for being alive, but there were still aspects of my experience I did not quite have a handle on. I needed to talk with others who had perhaps experienced something similar, especially about disturbing scenes they had witnessed. So I turned to people I knew and respected and to published accounts of some other Christians who had come back from the dead with memories of their experience to share.

Encouragement from Others Who Have Come Back

Thinking about how Teresa has changed since that day in April 2006, I see her appreciating life much more. We both do, and we both have realized how quickly life can end. You can be here one second and another second you can be gone. So get right with God now. That's the main message I'd like to pass on to everyone.

—Ronnie Simmons

I want to live the way my mom is living now. She has a bigger vision now, doesn't get bothered by the little things. I want to live my life every day like something could happen. I pray more, I try to be a better Christian. Nobody knows what's going to happen to us. After seeing all this and being a part of it, it's still so easy to get caught up in our daily chores. I won't say I think about this every day, but every so often I stop and say, I want to enjoy these colts and love the horses that I take care of, not just make it a job and rush through. It's what I do and what God has given me to do, but I want to enjoy it and be just more laid back.

—Jared Simmons

It's time for me to stop for a minute to make something very clear. I am a milkmaid, a farmer's wife, mother, and grandmother. I'm not an Anna, the New Testament prophetess in Luke 2 who recognized the child Jesus as the Messiah and who spent her days worshipping, fasting, and praying at the temple. Though I love to read my Bible, I am a woman who often communes with God through doing—as I milk the cows, bake a cake, or feed my grandsons. I'm not the kind who typically has visions or hears voices.

Yet I never doubted that what I saw was from God. Something that continues to impress me is how many doctors say short term memory is almost always affected by the kind of trauma I went through. Short term memory is very fragile and someone who has been clinically dead as I was will often either have some degree of brain damage or memory loss when revived.

I didn't. I think God wanted me to keep my memory of the time I was a witness to what I saw. I can't tell you the number of times I've tried to convince myself this was all due to lack of oxygen or medication. You may have thought that very thing as you have read my story. It would be so much easier for me to accept the memories I carry if I believed that. Then I would never have to face the fact that I really witnessed such a horrible place or saw the distress the people on that road were under. I would not have to feel compelled to share it. I would not have to risk what people might think about me. But I am convinced I am accountable to finish my work He sent me back here to do.

I did not need someone to validate what I had seen. What I needed was someone to help me further interpret and understand from a biblical perspective and framework what it meant. Pastor Ed and Eileen had already been of great help. Next I spoke with Wes Grove, an evangelist in our area, someone whose spiritual walk I respected. He had just read the book *Twenty-Three Minutes in Hell* (Charisma House, 2006) by Bill Wiese. He encouraged me to read it. "Maybe it will give you some understanding," he concluded.

The next day I called our local Christian bookstore and ordered the book. I had not read much on the subject of hell.

In a few days, the store called me to tell me that my book had arrived. I couldn't wait to read it.

I got the book and read it in one day. It was an amazing story of a vision of hell that God had given the author. I knew I had to talk to Bill Wiese. I noticed an e-mail address in the book, so I wrote a short account of what had happened to me and sent it with my phone number. Later that evening, his wife sent a reply. She told me in the e-mail that her husband would call me at a specific time, and I could share a full account of my story then.

The next afternoon, Bill Wiese called. I told him how much I appreciated his boldness in sharing what he had been allowed to see. (I could well understand by now the boldness it takes to share something so far outside the realm of common experience.) I had written a little of my story in my e-mail to him and I continued filling in the details. I knew from the very first I didn't have to be reluctant to tell him everything, because here was someone who would understand.

As I shared a full account of what had happened to me, he listened quietly on the other end. I spared no details. Here was a man who had seen grotesque figures in hell, had felt the fear and the pain that hell contains; he would understand. When I shared about the place where I stood and witnessed the multitude of people before me with terror-filled faces, I expressed my concern about not knowing the location of this place.

He suggested that maybe what I saw was the road to hell. It appeared to be going only one way and the people were being pushed along in one direction. Maybe the spiritual beings were ushering them into hell.

My heart nearly stopped. Now why hadn't I thought about that? I wondered.

Bill shared a quotation from Dr. Lester Sumrall that he also has in his book. Dr. Sumrall had a vision of the road that leads to hell:

> God lifted me up until I was looking down upon that uncountable multitude of humankind. He took me far down the highway until I saw the end of the road. It ended abruptly at a tower above a bottomless inferno. When the tremendous unending procession of people came to the end of the highway, I could see them falling off into eternity. As they neared the pit and saw the fate that awaited them, I could see their desperate but vain struggle to push back against the unrelenting pressure of those to the rear. The great surging river of humanity swept them ever forward. God opened my ears to hear the screams of damned souls sinking into Hell, I could see their faces distorted with terror. Their hands flailed wildly, clawing at the air (quoted by Wiese, 95).

The end of the road. . .an unending procession of people. . .Now this was beginning to make sense. I had seen a portion of the road that leads to hell. That thought kept tumbling through my brain over and over.

Wow, how come I hadn't thought about that? I kept wondering. Later that evening as I was putting away laundry, I really wasn't thinking about anything in particular when I recalled Jesus' words in Matthew 7:13–14:

> "Enter through the narrow gate. For wide is the gate and broad is the road that leads to destruction, and many enter through it. But small is the gate and narrow the road that leads to life, and only a few find it."

God just dropped that Scripture into my mind. It was as though He was confirming what Bill Wiese had just suggested to me.

I also read Don Piper's book, *Ninety Minutes in Heaven* (with Cecil Murphey, Revell, 2004). One of the similarities to my own experience that I found in Piper's account is the way he was greeted in heaven by family members. I stopped to think about how special this is. A loving God has the ones we held dearest in our earthly life come to greet us as we enter our eternal life. I had never thought about the unique significance of God doing that. What a personalized welcoming touch to have us greeted by the ones we loved! It's one more reason for us to pray for our families, as I think about it now. (A side note: When I was thinking of how to tell my story, Cecil Murphey, who collaborated with Don Piper in the writing of his story, encouraged me to write my own account.)

Each of these accounts by other Christians was an encouragement to me. I have since talked with other believers who have had similar experiences to mine, and what I saw meshes with what they have seen. "Test the spirits," the apostle says in 1 John 4:1, and part of that process is making sure any new truth revealed to us is in sync with what the Bible teaches. Mine is, all the way.

God continued to move in the hearts of people in our region through what we shared with them. In the following months, Ronnie and I began receiving invitations to speak at many churches. Some of the local newspapers heard of our story and published accounts of what had happened. I was impressed that even in a secular newspaper the name of Jesus was printed. God's miracle was told. Later the next year, a nationally published magazine ran a story about my experience. I am still astonished at how God is still getting my story told.

In the past three years, we've been invited to share our story in many churches. One of the latest invitations at the writing of this book was from the little white country church that I visited with my friend Donna as a teenager, where I gave my life to Christ. (God works in surprising ways!)

It is always amazing that God gives his grace to me as I share, as I still tend to be very apprehensive about getting in front of people. I can't say that I will ever be comfortable doing this, but I am completely willing to leave my comfort zone and tell my story if it means even one soul spared from that road. When I look back and think of my slim, slim chance of survival and then to know where God took me, I have to say, "Why not?" I'm not supposed to even be alive. God did a tremendous miracle. He defied all medical explanations and brought me back because He wants His people to know there is a hell.

I still continue to be shocked at how little hell is discussed in churches today. Worse yet, people are told there is no hell. They are told that God is too loving to send anyone there. It sounds so good, doesn't it?

Here's the truth: God sends no one to hell; people make that decision. To not make a decision for Christ is in itself a decision. God gives so many opportunities on this side of life, but people keep rejecting Him. He says in Rev. 3:20: "Here I am, I stand at the door and knock. If anyone hears my voice and opens the door I will come in." But too often the unopened door is as clear a rejection as one can make.

God wants us to know that hell is real. We are living in the last days. None of us know our last day here on this earth. I surely didn't think my life was about to end on April 10, 2006, but I came close that day and by the grace and mercy of God, I'm alive. However, had I died, I know where my eternal home is. There are only two places after this life: heaven and hell. It is a choice; we determine our future destination.

Hell is real. I can't say it enough times. I never doubted its existence before, and I definitely do not now. Some may question why God gave me this vision. To better explain this, I will quote a portion from *Twenty-Three Minutes in Hell*:

> I believe that the only reason God took me to Hell was to draw attention to His word on the subject. It is not that He needs my help, or anybody else's. However, I believe time is getting short, and there are some unusual things God is doing in the earth today to help people awaken to the truth. He is imploring people to listen to His word. This is not a condemning message, but a warning message. God does not want anyone to go down the heavily traveled road that many are on (98).

God tells us that He does not want anyone to perish (2 Peter 3:9). He loves us so much but He gives us all the decision to choose Him or not to choose Him. Isn't it sad to think our Creator waits patiently for His creation to come back to Him and then He is rejected? Remember, not to choose is to choose. It is our decision.

Many years ago, I had a conversation with a daughter of a college professor. She was attending college at the time, and she made the comment that one of her college professors had said many of the stories in the Bible are mere fables. She told me that she believed this to be true. She concluded with, "Whoever believes these stories sure has a shallow intelligence." I felt the Holy Spirit grieve inside of me. This lady was such a brilliant woman, but she based her viewpoint of the Bible on human reasoning or intellect.

I have shared my story many times in churches. I'm always amazed at how people try to put God on their level of understanding. God and His word can't be "reasoned out." Jesus tells us unless we become like little children, we will never enter the kingdom of God (Matthew 18:3). It is all about faith. We cannot base our decision on human intellect. Only through His Spirit can an understanding be revealed.

Certainly the world is going to call Jesus' teaching shallow, or maybe childish. Why should we want to become less sophisticated, less able to "stand on our own two feet," "pull ourselves up by our own bootstraps," and be self-sufficient in that good old American way? The world asks, "Why become like children?"

Because children accept in faith. They trust. They are innocent. They don't worry. This mind-set is a foreign concept to the world. It just seems too simplistic, and yet, it is the very place where God calls us to be. We have to change our thinking. We are so accustomed to doing things the way we feel we will best be accepted in society. We do things out of habit or because we value other people's opinion of us too much.

God calls us away from that. He says, "Don't rely on your way of thinking. Lay down your life the way you've been living it. Come trust in me and let me take care of things." (See Proverbs 3:5, Romans 12:2, and Psalms 25:4-5.) He picks us up as a loving, caring parent and does just what He promises. That is where we have a relationship with our creator. He tells us there is only one way to Him. He gave His only Son as a sacrifice. He exhorts us that if we "… confess with your mouth Jesus is Lord, and believe in your heart that God raised Him from the dead, you will be saved" (Romans 10:9).

One road to Heaven… to know Jesus Christ as our Lord and Savior. One road to hell…never to receive Him as our Lord and Savior. It is that simple; the choice is clearly yours.

Let's Throw Away the Crutches

As I continue to share my story I'm impressed to find many people who carry crutches in life. They are hurting. Life has stung them. They need to find something to take away the sting. These crutches might work for a while.

As a society we have learned instant gratification. We want the pain gone, and we want it gone now! Sadly, people turn to alcohol, drugs, food, sexual sins, money, shopping, whatever crutches they can find to help soothe. Often they grab onto multiple crutches. When one crutch quits propping them up, people turn to another, and then another, until one day the "fix" quits working because it has become dull. In desperation, what do they reach out for then?

Unfortunately, we read about many suicides because someone has "reached the end of his rope." It is a very dark place to come to. However, it is at this place that God is waiting. He has all the answers. He takes that stinger out, picks up the stung ones and lovingly nurtures us back. He has waited all along, knowing that one day we will reach this point, and it is when we are at rock bottom that we have to look up. He offers a new life. He offers hope. He offers a new road. The choice is ours.

I've often noticed how many people hold onto the crutch that if one is active enough in church, he or she is going to make it to heaven. Being good and serving on all the "right" committees and organizations do not translate into salvation. We need to use the gifts that God has given each of us and help our fellow believers, but just "doing" and being a good person will not save us. When Christ talks in Scripture about many coming to Him and saying, "Lord, Lord" and He answers them with the words, "Get away from me, I never *knew* you," He is saying that these people never had a relationship with Him. They were busy doing things and they felt their actions were for a worthy cause, but who were they really doing things for? People like to impress other people. How sad. They go through life being busy, trying to look good to others, and missing out entirely. They miss the only way to heaven—a relationship with Jesus.

When we live in that relationship, we can never go wrong. We find our direction in life. We discover why we are here. God says in Jeremiah 29:11: "For I know the plans I have for you . . . plans to give you hope and a future." We realize that the true simplicity of walking in His ways is the answer, no matter if the world calls this way of life shallow. It is the only way to true lasting peace and happiness, and it is the only way that leads us to heaven. Matthew 7:13 says it is a narrow passageway. It is so sad that many people choose the wide road. Until they decide to throw down the crutches and take the fork in the road that the Lord offers many times in their lives, they will find themselves on the road right into hell, a horrible, horrible place.

God allowed this milkmaid to see a portion of this road. Why did He choose me? Why didn't He choose some well-known figure? Often God will do this. He uses people and things of little recognition to let His mighty acts show through.

Again, I believe God does this as He sees a willing vessel, one ready to use the gifts God has given him or her as a member of the body of Christ. I've known for quite awhile that God has given me a gift of compassion. Often, both before and after my out-of-body experience, when someone has been going through some type of distress I have felt such deep, deep sympathy for that person. I want to "fix it" somehow, but I have learned the only way a situation can be remedied is through prayer and through God's hand.

I am confident God knew I would use the gift of compassion He had already given me after I returned to my place as a milkmaid. He knew that when I came back after seeing what I had seen, I would not be able to just "let it rest." My deep feelings of sorrow for those poor souls on that road will not let me keep this experience to myself. I feel at times that if I could shout this from the mountaintops, I would!

There is a real hell, people. The world beyond this world is much more real than this one. We are truly just passing through. This world seems so, so temporary to me now. That spiritual world somehow seems more real than this world. I don't know how to explain that any better. Psalms 39:4-7 says it so well:

> "Show me, O Lord, my life's end and the number of my days; let me know how fleeting is my life. You have made my days a mere handbreadth; the span of my years is as nothing before you. Each man's life is but a breath. Selah. Man is a mere phantom as he goes to and fro: He bustles about, but only in vain; he heaps up wealth, not knowing who will get it. But now, Lord, what do I look for? My hope is in you."

Our lives here are so temporary. I'm often amazed at how bogged down we get with minute details in life, and we often go through much of our lives so fully focused on the physical aspect that we give little thought to the "hereafter," our future eternal destination. This busy lifestyle is a huge tool Satan uses to keep us from ever growing in Christ, or sadly, ever coming to know our Savior. Colossians 3:2 tells us, to "Set your mind on things above, not on earthly things."

None of us has a guarantee that we have a long life ahead of us. We do not know when our time will come to and end here on this earth. None of us. We often go through life fully expecting to reach a ripe age of eighty-five, ninety, ninety-five if we are lucky. How can we be sure we will live that long?

What Road Will You Take?

Today is the day of salvation. Can you honestly go another minute if there is any unrest right now in your spirit about your eternal destination? Do you know Jesus Christ, the Son of God? Acts 4:12 says: "Salvation is found in no one else, for there is no other name under Heaven given to men by which we must be saved." Jesus is the only way to heaven.

Childlike faith? You betcha. Why not put to rest all the opinions, thoughts, habits, intellect, and reasoning you've ever had to try in order to ignore His call on your life? He is calling you. He is knocking on the door of your heart right now. If I could somehow be with you right now, precious reader, I would. I wish I could personally share the details of that road to hell. It's no place you will ever, ever want to be.

Right now, you have a chance. Right now, you have a choice. Precious person, make that choice now. Get off the road you are on. God is offering you a new road today. He is reaching out. He is waiting lovingly, patiently. He does not want you to perish. He doesn't want you on that road, shocked and hopeless, someday. It's your choice. Make a decision for him today.

One day, I pray that this milkmaid will see you on that road that leads right into heaven. One day, I pray you will be greeted by your saved loved ones with their arms open, ready to embrace you. But best of all, I pray you will be there with me as we hear the precious words of our Lord and Savior: "Well done, good and faithful servant," and be fully embraced in His loving arms. Which road do you choose today?

Sinner's Prayer

Never believe you are so bad that God will not accept you. Never believe it is too late to ask Him into your life. Never believe God doesn't love you. They are all lies that Satan has used to convince you. God is full of mercy and love. He wants you today. Humble yourself as a little child and go to Him now and pray.

> God, I admit I am a sinner. I've messed up. I acknowledge my sins before you now and I ask your forgiveness. I believe you sent your Son, Jesus, to die for me. He took my place. I believe in Jesus and I believe He arose and went to Heaven. I repent today and I put my trust in Jesus Christ. In Jesus' name I pray.
> Amen

You have allowed the Lord into your heart. This is a huge decision on your part! Right now, heaven is rejoicing. God has been waiting on you. Find a Bible-believing church to attend, tell someone that walks closely to God what decision you've made, and read His word. Find a translation that is easy to understand. A Christian book store is often helpful. God has a plan for you, precious one. I don't know you, but I've been praying for lost souls. This is the best decision you've ever made in your life. Now start walking on that road that leads to Heaven. God will lead you as you walk with Him.

Teresa Simmons
May 1, 2009

Epilogue
In Memoriam: Andrew Wesley Simmons

Once again, our family has been reminded of the brevity of life. On Monday, Memorial Day, May 25, 2009, my nephew, Andrew Wesley Simmons, age 16, my brother Mark's middle son, accidentally shot himself in the chest while cleaning his gun.

The pain that has hit our family due to the suddenness of death is beyond words. We relived once again the grief of burying one so young. Over one thousand people mourned his death and attended his funeral and memorial services. He was a well-liked kid in the community as well as in his school.

This occurred the very week I was finishing this book. As my mind has reflected back on what happened, heaven has seemed a little closer.

As I have related my story, I have tried to drive home the truth that we are here one minute and gone the next. Had I not come back, that would have been the case with me, and it certainly was the case for Mark. And now Andrew is gone, too.

Andrew had been swimming and camping with friends and his little brother just a couple of hours before he died, never realizing how events would unfold soon after he got home. His young life is gone—gone from us, but he is forever with our heavenly Father and back in his daddy's arms.

I know this with assurance because Andrew was a believer in Jesus Christ. My prayer as you read my story is that you will have that same assurance before you leave this earth.

Made in the USA
Charleston, SC
27 January 2010